PRAISE FOR TOM SNELL'S
BEOWULF'S APPRENTICE
A Cardiac Patient's

"Congratulations on this wonderful ... ...ly
engaged and I couldn't put it down. ...... are just beginning to
explore the role of a patient's spiritual life in surviving major surgery.
Beowulf's Apprentice can become part of this ongoing
conversation in our culture."
Vito Victor—writer

"A moving account of life and death, of fear and courage, and of
entering the Mystery which sustains all of Life. My fall and its
repercussions were much more painful than I anticipated, and your
words about fear and depression and the journey to the other side
were wonderfully helpful. The poetry and the journeys into the
Unconscious open out inviting possibilities."
Bill Cane—author, Director of IF

Beowulf's Apprentice is about searching for that space where we
accept ourselves and life's challenges by finding creative ways to
cope. Snell encourages doing the "detective work" in unusual places
for most of us, taking risks, learning to reach out for support.
Whether you are unsettled about work, marriage, or life-threatening
health problems, Snell has much to say to you.
Susan Samuels Drake
(Susan is author of *Fields of Courage: Remembering Cesar Chavez & the People
Whose Labor Feeds Us* (Many Names Press, 1999), a poetic memoir based on her
31-year-long friendship with the labor leader. Her essays and poems
appear in a variety of anthologies.)

"We've all confronted life-threatening illness and death, but seldom to
the extent experienced by the author and his family. As he revisits these
experiences and invites us into his private life, his gifts of sensitivity,
self-exploration, narrative ability, and . . . in the end . . . wisdom draw us
into not only his life story, but our own. Along the way, we learn how making
peace with mortality is, at the same time, making peace with living."
Andrew Neher, psychologist

This extraordinary story takes the reader through one man's journey that plumbs the heights and depths of experience. Kant talks about the effort of existence. This is existential effort in the face of suffering and mourning in the extreme, witnessed by the shaman's effort of self-transcendence and luminous disclosure of the meaning of it all. The suffering and death of his son anticipates the suffering and rebirth of his own open-heart surgery. The author internalizes these ordeals and conquers them.

Paul Lee, STB, PhD—author, university professor, pastor, herbalist, and homeless advocate

"I admire Tom Snell's courage, honesty, vulnerability, and resourcefulness. He has truly transformed the experience of a medical crisis into an opportunity for living more deeply and authentically. In *Beowulf's Apprentice,* he writes: 'Would this experience work me, like the smithy works the iron at the hot forge, moving me further into my humanity?' That is, perhaps, the most essential question to ask ourselves in facing any painful or frightening life event. And the answer in Tom's case is a resounding *yes!*"

Ellen Bass—Poet and Author

Beowulf's Apprentice

A Cardiac Patient's Spiritual Memoir

Tom Snell

To order additional copies of this book, contact:
Xlibris Corporation
1-888-795-4274
www.Xlibris.com
Orders@Xlibris.com
45943

Contents

PART THREE
Paradiso

APPENDICES

ACKNOWLEDGEMENTS

There is a lifetime of people to thank who either supported this writing directly or who taught me some of the life lessons shared within these covers. I cannot begin to name them all, but these stand out: my first wife Julie whose wisdom and strength got our family through two early crises; my second wife Delia for her steadfastness and patience; my friend Mary Ann Peterson who listened again and again as I struggled through my search for transformation and meaning; my co-counselor Janet Merrick whose skills helped me express my fear and grief; Cathy Jarosz who nurtured my spirit; the surgeons and nurses without whose genius and care I might not be alive today; Harvey Jackens, Michael Harner, David Whyte and others whose writings and teachings healed and inspired me over the years; the many friends who gave me feedback on my first writing attempts, my editors Susan Drake and Vito Victor, and finally the wide circle of family and friends who loved and sustained me through it all. Without these people none of this would have been possible.

This book is dedicated to all my children,
but especially to my son Timothy—(1970-1975)

Disclaimers

I do not claim accuracy in my description of medical terms, issues, or procedures. For those you should check with your doctor or a good medical library. This book is about my experience, and may or may not be medically accurate.

There are places throughout this book where I have changed people's names or revised stories for reasons of privacy and confidentiality.

PART ONE

Inferno

Midway in the journey of our life
I came to myself in a dark wood,
for the straight way was lost.

Ah, how hard it is to tell
the nature of that wood, savage, dense and harsh—
the very thought of it renews my fear!

It is so bitter death is hardly more so.
But to set forth the good I found
I will recount the other things I saw.

The Inferno, Canto I
—*Dante Alighieri*, 1265-1321
—Translators *Robert and Jean Hollander*

CHAPTER 1

I Enter the Dark Wood

There was no hint of crisis that morning: no premonitory dreams, no warning cries from the birds pecking at our garden feeders outside my window, no intimation of the nightmare that was about to invade my life. Nor had I expected any. Instead, I awoke refreshed. With the sun already streaming into my room, I got up, made coffee, and drove to the nearby beach for my daily walk. When I got home, I ate breakfast with my wife, Delia, then settled in for a good read in the easy chair that overlooks our garden.

A half hour later my reading was interrupted by the slam of a car door, followed by a distant "Where's Gramps?" I rushed to my desk and pretended to be busy at the computer. Seconds later I heard the door to my room sigh open ever so quietly followed by tiny footsteps tiptoeing across the carpet. I swung my chair around with a "Who's there?", but no one was in sight. "Who's hiding from me?" Soon I saw a foot followed by a leg followed by a nine-year old girl giggling her way out from behind the couch. She stood up, grabbed my hand and started pulling me out of my chair and toward the door.

"Come read Harry Potter!"

"Sierra, what's the magic word?"

"Please."

As I started to follow her, she swung around to face me, grabbed me around the waist and placed both her feet on top of mine. Then, pulling me slightly off balance, she started moving us in a comical lockstep toward the main part of the house. Now we were both giggling so hard we could hardly stay standing. As I fell gasping onto the living room couch, she jumped into my lap, thrust *The Chamber of Secrets* into my hands and again said, "Please read."

Delia, who had been watching the whole exchange while fixing lunch, said, "But Sierra, we've already listened to this one twice. You want Gramps to read it again?"

"Yes—please, please, please, *please.* Read it again!"

So, with our granddaughter in my lap, I began.

Clearly life had improved since my retirement. The previous ten years had been stressful, with long commutes and ten hour work days, but now retirement provided a lot more free time. Not only was Delia's granddaughter teaching me to be playful again, but I was finding all sorts of new interests and opportunities. Friends had introduced me to shamanism and the shamanic journey, and more recently I had discovered the cello, both intoxicating challenges. I had never felt so free. Now I had the leisure to investigate who I was, to explore, to find what fed and nurtured me. It was an exciting time, and I was only just getting started.

That afternoon I drove to my doctor's for my annual checkup. After taking my blood pressure, he pressed his stethoscope to my chest in two or three places, then did it again. With the third attempt, he frowned, stepped back, and sighed.

"I'm going to send you to a cardiologist. Your prolapsed mitral valve sounds much worse."

"What do you mean, 'worse'? There's nothing wrong with me. I've been feeling great." As I spoke, tension began to build between my shoulder blades, and my gut turned leaden with dread.

"Well, it's changed. Until now the small bit of leakage we've heard over the years has been insignificant, but this is different. You've got to see a specialist."

Outwardly I must have appeared calm. I asked a few questions, got the name of a cardiologist, and made an appointment. But inwardly my heart wanted to pound its way out of my chest and a very scared voice was whispering, *What's this? Something's wrong with my heart? This can't be happening!* By the time I got home, I felt as though I had stepped into Dante's dark and ominous wood.

Three days later I saw the cardiologist. After a quick exam, he ordered a stress echocardiogram. That didn't seem so menacing—I had had one of those before—so I went ahead. Two afternoons later I found myself with half a dozen wires stuck to my chest while walking a steep and rapidly moving treadmill. Every minute or so the technician would increase the speed until I was gasping so hard I could barely respond to her questions. Finally, when I thought my lungs would burst with the effort, she stopped the treadmill and told me to quickly lie down on the examination table. Sliding her cold instrument over the left side of my chest, she began to extract the images that would decide my fate.

"What do you think?" I asked.

"There's definitely some valve leakage, but you'll have to see your doctor again. He'll do the diagnosis."

That night I hardly slept, dozing and waking so many times that I moved to the couch so I wouldn't disturb Delia. The next day wasn't much better. I tried to sit at my desk and write letters, but every so often I would jump up and pace the room. Three times I drove to the store to do unnecessary errands—anything to get out of the house and away from the thoughts that were spinning out of control: *Will I have to have heart surgery? What if I get a stroke? How serious is this?* Finally I saw the cardiologist again.

"I looked at your echo, and . . ."

"Well, what did you see?" I interrupted.

"It shows quite a bit of leakage," he said, a tinge of annoyance in his voice, "but I need to see more detail to know what to recommend. I want to admit you to the hospital so we can do a cardiac catheterization."

Oh damn, I thought. *Not the hospital. I hate hospitals.* Then, "What's a cardiac catheterization?"

"It's where we run a tube to your heart and inject a dye so we can see your heart in more detail."

"How long does it take?"

"It's takes most of a day. We'll use the major artery in your leg as a pathway to the heart. Once there, we can release a dye so we can take x-ray pictures of your heart at work."

"Didn't we just do that with the stress echo?"

"Yes, but this gives much more detail. We can also check the blood flow through your heart arteries to see if there's any blockage."

"Oh," I replied.

I was so stunned I could barely make the appointment. On the drive home everything felt heavy. More horrible thoughts ran round and round in my head, like a dozen snakes chasing their tails. They kept hissing, *What if the doctor pokes that tube through the artery wall and into something vital? What if he can't close off the artery? What if I bleed to death?*

Somehow, with Delia's help, I got through the next four days, and the following morning she drove me to the hospital for my 7:00AM admission. As we climbed out of the car, she said, "Are you sure you don't want me to stay?"

"No. It's okay. It will be long and boring. I'll call you when it's done. You can pick me up then."

After signing various hospital documents, a nurse led me deep into the bowels of the building. The further we went the more effort it took to drag my reluctant body after the rapidly advancing nurse. When we reached the treatment room, she motioned me to a chair. "The doctor has been delayed a few minutes—please wait." I looked around. *What is it about that white door?*

*   *   *

It's the summer of 1972. I'm in a hospital in Keene, New Hampshire where I've been sitting and staring for a long time at a similar white door. Here there is fear and pain seeping under the sill. On the other side two nurses are holding down my eight-year old son, Christopher, so the doctor can give him his biweekly infusion of chemotherapy. For nearly half an hour I wait, feeling his anguish and shamed by my inability to help. While I sit rigidly upright, my sweat-soaked shirt dries to the chair-back. Every so often I bend forward and place my head in my hands, elbows on my knees, trying to relieve the tension of the long wait. Each time I move, my glued shirt rips away from the chair-back with a soft 'ziiit' sound.

Finally the door opens and one of the nurses comes out leading Chris by the hand. Without a word he joins me, his silence an accusation. Like an automaton I get up and we start the journey home.

It was thirty years ago that my first wife, Julie, and I first learned about Christopher's rare tumor. For two years we battled his cancer and eventually won. But though the cancer never returned, the scars of his fear lingered. While he was sick, Christopher had desperately needed to be held, to cry, to pound me in his fear and frustration, and to scream his young heart out. But this was the one thing I could not give him. I grew up in a family that was unfamiliar with physical affection, uncomfortable with feelings, far more at ease with things of the intellect. Hugging and holding were not our strengths. Christopher's tears were cries for help exactly where I was most helpless and inadequate.

Clearly I had needed assistance, but that, too, was a problem. In my childhood I had been taught to solve all problems myself and I had become good at it. But I also remember getting stuck, usually on some particularly complex homework problem. At first I tried asking my Dad for help. His response was always, "You should work it out for yourself." What seemed obvious to him would be a deep conundrum for me, a Gordian knot I couldn't unravel.

It was only years after Chris' illness, when my brother called me early one morning to say that he had heard on the radio that Dad had won the Nobel Prize[1] for solving one of the most complex puzzles in biology—the genetics of the immune system—that I finally understood what an accomplished genius my father had been. A very shy and unassuming man, even at home, few outside his field knew what he was doing. He had been so modest that, when the prize was announced, the neighbors thought he had gotten an award for the vegetables he was always giving away from his backyard garden. When he died in 1996 at the age of 92, my brother and I had to go through the house to prepare it for sale. Piled in a dusty old box in the attic were more than a dozen prestigious awards and honors[2]: awards from the Wolf Foundation, the Czechoslovak Academy of Sciences, and the National Library of Medicine; elected to the French and American Academies of Science and to the British Transplantation and Immunology Societies . . . . The list went on and on. All these had been hidden away, as though my Dad's genius was some family skeleton to be locked in the proverbial closet.

Throughout my childhood all the outward signs had been of an ordinary father. Like so many dads, he drove to work in the morning, came home in time for supper, and got a regular paycheck in the mail. Like a good son, I thought I should be like him. Completely unaware that my father was

---

[1]   It was "for discovery of the Major histocompatibility complex genes which encode cell surface molecules important for the immune system's distinction between self and non-self" that my dad shared the 1980 Nobel Prize in physiology and medicine with Baruj Benacerraf of Harvard and Jean Dausset of France.

[2]   See Appendix A—George D. Snell

anything but ordinary, I had no idea what an impossible task I had set for myself. I remember one event in particular.

I'm in the fifth grade, preparing for the spring science fair. I've chosen genetics as my topic. This seems to make sense. My dad's a geneticist and genetics is a science, so of course I'll write about that.

Using Dad's Encyclopedia Britannica, I find three or four highly technical articles on the subject. The words on the page are so familiar, so much a part of the background buzz of our household, that I feel reassured. I "know" them all: gene, chromosome, allele, genotype, phenotype, hybrid, linkage, inbred strain, recombination . . . . But as I start to write in my own words, it suddenly becomes difficult. Why is this so hard? Dad does this—why can't I? I struggle for days, finally typing eight single-spaced pages on Dad's old Underwood.

The next day, as I stand alone by my exhibit, I feel sweat dampen my shirt, even though the room is cool. When the judge comes by, I watch him lean across the table and peer at the closely-spaced type-written text. He reads a line, pauses, adjusts his glasses, reads some more. After two paragraphs he sighs, steps back, gives me the strangest look, and moves on. *What's wrong? I've worked so hard! Something's not right.* I feel the blood rush to my face and want to run away in shame. Instead, I stand there frozen, too mortified to speak or move.

Looking back, I realize I had written gibberish. I had confused familiarity with understanding and had done little more than reshuffle the words in ways that didn't make sense or that parroted the encyclopedia. Wanting so much to be like my "ordinary" Dad, and with no guidance, I had stepped in way over my head. A more appropriate project might have been something as simple (and as profound) as putting garden soil in a cup, planting a few pea seeds, adding water, then reporting what happened.

Growing up with these unconscious, self-imposed, expectations of brilliant accomplishment, I soon became too ashamed of my limitations to ever ask for help. Eventually, when faced with a problem I couldn't solve, I became paralyzed and did nothing.

And so it had been with Chris' illness. I hadn't known how to give him what he needed and was too ashamed to ask for help, so I had become frozen. It was in that frozen state that I took him again and again to that torture chamber where toxic chemicals were dripped into his veins to save his life. Physically I was there, driving the car, walking with him into the waiting room, but emotionally and spiritually I was withdrawn into a deep shell of despair. At the age of eight, he had to endure these treatments alone.

Through all his treatments, Julie and I struggled to maintain some semblance of a normal life. Not only did we both have full-time teaching jobs, but we were trying to raise three other children while making dozens of two-hour drives to Massachusetts General Hospital for two surgeries, weeks of radiation, and follow-ups on the chemotherapy. Meanwhile, for two years, Chris inhaled our fears and made them his own.

*   *   *

"Mr. Snell, please get undressed and put on this hospital gown. I'll be back in a few minutes." Shaking my head to clear away these ancient memories, I struggled to come back to the treatment room and get ready for the heart catheterization.

Now that it was time, all my anticipatory fears evaporated. I watched closely as the surgeon numbed my groin, made the cut, and slid the catheter into my artery. The biologist in me was fascinated. On the computer screen next to my bed, I could see the image of a thin black tube snaking its way through the central part of my body and into the very center of my heart. There it kept releasing puffs of a dark substance that, for brief moments, revealed the heart's inner structure in finest detail. I could see its chambers squeezing and releasing, its valves opening and closing, pushing most of the blood onward to do its vital work throughout my body. But I could also see that the damaged valve wasn't working properly. It was torn and leaking. When the heart squeezed, it pushed too much blood the wrong way through the valve, sending it backward toward my lungs instead of forward to nourish my body.

When the doctor finished, the hardest part was to lie completely still for the six or eight hours it took for the entry point into my artery to heal enough so that Delia could drive me home.

My next doctor's visit was to discuss the results. As he began to talk about the procedure, I flashed back again to our son. This time I saw him lying on our living room couch, a bowl and washcloth on a low table beside him, his small body racked with dry heaves from the chemotherapy. Meanwhile, as though from a great distance, I heard phrases like "congestive heart failure", "eventually fatal", "single by-pass", and "you must see a heart valve surgeon." I must have been holding my breath most of the time, because when the doctor stopped speaking, I felt as though I might turn blue. When I stood up, I felt faint and grasped the edge of the exam table to steady myself. The doctor had turned toward his notes on the counter next to him and didn't notice, but I was feeling distinctly unwell. As I staggered out the door, the doctor said, "Make sure you call that number I gave you. He's a good surgeon."

As I started home, I turned up the car radio to drown out a flood of gloomy thoughts, and for the next few days a great deal of energy went to keeping this interloper voice deep in the shadows of my mind. But he persisted, lurking half-hidden around the corner, almost but not quite out of hearing.

I had always been healthy and had never had anything more than my tonsils out. Like a teenager, I still felt immortal. Despite Christopher's illness, things like cancer and heart problems always happened to someone else's body, never to mine. Rather than face the problem, it felt much safer to get busy, pretending that life could go on as before, that nothing had changed, and that the true and terrible nature of the crisis didn't exist. I wanted to avoid the issue so completely, I didn't even call my three grown children to tell them what was happening.

But I couldn't hold it off forever. Eventually this threat would force me to look at my world in a whole new way and make me face my biggest fears.

CHAPTER 2

Facts or Feelings, Who Rules?

Lord, I am but a flit of a butterfly wing,
One half-stroke in a world of monsoons,
One brief spurt of breath—and my time will be gone,
Lost amongst a sea of nameless faces,
And other fragile, frantic wings.
I will disappear as the single drop in the ocean does,
Or one star in the heavens.
And, Lord, though I understand none of it,
I rejoice, and would have it no other way.

—Rachel Medlock

E verything was happening too quickly. I barely knew my cardiologist, a young man who, from my advanced age, seemed fresh out of high school. Yet now he had told me I should see a heart surgeon and recommended someone at a hospital two hours away. As he gave me a phone number and told me to make an appointment, all sorts of doubts started to rise up like hungry beasts from the thicket of my fears: *Is this kid competent enough to know who is the best surgeon, the one who will literally be holding my life in his hands during surgery? Is he giving me the best possible advice or is he just promoting a friend from medical school? Even worse, is he getting a kickback, choosing the surgeon who would pay him the most?*

Despite these doubts, I called and was able to get an appointment two weeks later. Meanwhile I put on my detective's hat and started my own search. Although my condition was critical in the long term, there was no rush to an immediate surgery so I had time to explore. I scanned the web, called friends, and networked. Everywhere I looked this surgeon's reputation was excellent. A rating system for hospitals and surgeons placed him at the top, he did about 300 heart valves a year or nearly one a day giving him a huge reservoir of experience, and a recent article in a San Francisco newspaper featured his stellar work. I could hardly go wrong. I will call him Dr. Valve-a-Day.

Two weeks later, as Delia and I took the long drive to the initial office visit, my nervousness mounted. Half way there the traffic slowed to a crawl, and for forty-five minutes we waited for the highway patrol to clear an accident. A big boulder of anxiety in the center of my gut grew heavier, making my back ache and my shoulders tense. Finally, very late, we pulled into the parking lot.

As I sat for a moment letting the tension of the trip dissipate, Delia gently squeezed my hand. "It will be okay. I know how difficult doctors and hospitals have been for you, but hang in there. And don't forget, I'm here too—you're not doing this alone."

Inside, the entrance corridor was dark and gloomy, lit only by a few windows near the far end. An ugly gray carpet made it even more oppressive. There were no names on the doors, only suite numbers. Was this the right place? I looked at my notes—yes, Room 210.

We entered a waiting area that felt just as heavy. The receptionist sat closed off behind a glass wall trimmed with wide strips of chrome that radiated a metallic aura of brittle distance and unwelcome. After a long pause, she slid open her window with a questioning look. "Yes?"

"Hi, I'm Tom Snell and I had an appointment for 11:30. I'm sorry we're late, but we got stuck behind a big accident on the Interstate."

"Well, yes, you *are* late."

"I was hoping the doctor could fit us in sometime this afternoon. We've come a long way and it would be difficult to make a second trip. Would that be possible?"

Looking peeved, she responded, "You'll have to wait." Then she pointed to the chairs scattered around the room and abruptly closed the window.

There was nothing to do but sit . . . and sit . . . and sit. During our stay the aloof staff ignored us, making the wait even more difficult.

Two and a half hours and a missed lunch later, they finally called my name and we entered a large room with a huge desk and a seating area off to one side. The surgeon certainly looked the part. Tall, athletic, oozing a slick confidence, he strode across the room, shook hands brusquely, and motioned us to sit. Yes, he had looked at the tests my cardiologist had sent with me. Yes, it would most likely be a repair, but just in case, I would have to choose between an artificial valve or a pig valve as a replacement. Also, if I wanted, he could fix that atrial fibrillation I had been having with a Maze procedure. Then, looking at his watch, he shooed us out of his office with the instructions to set a surgery date with the staff out front. My mind clouded by fear and full of half-formed questions, I did as I was told. On our way out, the woman at the front desk told me to complete an Advance Medical Directive and bring it with me to surgery.

I was stunned and feeling intensely uncomfortable. I didn't like this guy. Could I let this stranger split open the armor of my rib cage and expose the most vital secrets of my heart? Just the thought made me want to wrap my arms across my chest and curl into a tiny ball. Even though his intention would be to repair the damage, I felt too exposed and vulnerable. And there was so much to consider, so many decisions to make.

Before this moment I had always been able to rely on my intellect and problem-solving abilities for making decisions. My father had spent his life in basic research, and my college and graduate school majors had been in the biological sciences. Rational thought was a place of comfort, a centerpiece of my life. All I needed were a few impartial facts and I could solve most problems to my satisfaction.

But now, my ability to rely on the facts (which were still saying, "Dr. Valve-a-Day is technically the best—he has golden hands—use him.") had abandoned me. Instead, the place deep inside that was becoming all too familiar was yelling *No—I don't think so!* Some primitive, animal-self had overruled my intelligence, making me very uneasy. Right or wrong it said, *I don't like him. I don't trust him; he doesn't care about me, doesn't care enough to fight for my survival. I am just another body to him, just another morning surgery to get done so he can buy his third Porsche.*

I drove home more confused than ever.

CHAPTER 3

The Wood Gets Darker

Suspended
I had grasped God's garment in the void
but my hand slipped
on the rich silk of it.
The 'everlasting arms' my sister loved to remember
must have upheld my leaden weight
from falling, even so,
for though I claw at empty air and feel
nothing, no embrace,
I have not plummetted.

—Denise Levertov

The surgeon hadn't told me anything about the two types of replacement valve that I might need, so the next day I went searching on the Internet. The chances were good that these valves would not be used—that the surgeon would be able to make the repair—but they wouldn't know until they were well inside my heart. I thought the choice between valves would be easy: learn a little about each and then pick one. I couldn't have been more wrong.

I started with the artificial valve. I soon found it would last forever. That seemed okay, but then I read on. To use this valve I would have to take daily doses of blood thinner to prevent clots. The thinner required nearly continuous monitoring—too little and I could get a clotting stroke—too much and I could bruise or bleed easily, making even small accidents potentially hazardous. The amount of thinning would be very sensitive to the amount of vitamin K in my blood. I would have to become very rigid about daily diet of green vegetables to keep that constant. All this for the rest of my life? It seemed like a lousy choice, so I looked up the pig valve.

"No medication required." That seemed good. Maybe I could go with the pig valve. "Lasts a few years, then requires a second open-heart surgery to replace the first one." I nearly fell out of my chair. Surgery again? If I was going to live past seventy-five or eighty, and I certainly planned to, this would be a lousy choice. Then, to really clinch the matter, I read, "Major surgery more risky in older patients."

What was I going to do? One chest surgery terrified me, two were inconceivable, but the possibility of stroke chipping away at my capabilities felt equally terrifying. These didn't feel like choices—they felt like potential death sentences.

I still knew nothing about the Maze procedure, so at my next cardiologist appointment I asked him.

"As you know, we discovered a few weeks ago that you've been having some occasional atrial fibrillation. This is not uncommon in someone your age."

"Yeah, the racing heart and fatigue."

"Yes. That's because your heart can't pump as well when it's in AF. AF can also cause blood clots, so after the surgery you will have to go on blood thinner to protect you from stroke."

Damn, I thought, *not blood thinner again.* "So what does this have to do with the Maze procedure?"

"In the Maze, a maze-like series of cuts are made in the atria of the heart to eliminate the fibrillation."

"Isn't that pretty drastic?" I said.

"Yes. Under normal circumstances it's done only where the fibrillation has become very severe. In your situation we wouldn't usually consider it—you have too mild a case. However, since your chest will already be open this time for the valve repair, adding the procedure is something to consider."

"Does this add any risk?" I asked. "If not, it seems that I should just go ahead and get it done. I hate the idea of a second surgery."

"Yes, it adds a measurable amount of risk. That's why we leave it up to you."

I hung up the phone. What should I do? Would the fibrillation get worse or better? Should I add this risk to my upcoming surgery or be on blood thinner for the rest of my life? I couldn't decide.

Looking back I realize that I had only seen these as bad choices. It wasn't that many years before that I would not have had any choices at all—no pig or artificial valves, no Maze procedure. A few years before that, no one had yet invented heart-lung machines or performed such a surgery. How lucky I had been to have *any* choice! But the tunnel vision of my fear and the way it amplified the negative aspects of each choice, hadn't allowed me to see that.

*   *   *

I had tentatively scheduled my surgery for as late in the summer as they would let me, August fifth, about three months away. My excuse had been that I didn't want to miss some important summer events. I also rationalized that I needed time to prepare, but I think my real motivation was to put everything off for as long as possible.

Now, with time on my hands, I put my analytical skills to work, trying to resolve the remaining decisions and make good choices. I learned everything I could about the types of valves, my heart, and the Maze procedure. I networked with nursing friends. I joined numerous chat rooms and bulletin board discussions, looking for anyone who had struggled with similar problems. What had they decided? How had they come to those decisions?

But the search for answers went on and on. Long before dawn, I would stagger to the kitchen in my pajamas, make a huge mug of coffee and return to my desk, still blurry-eyed with sleep. Within moments of sitting at the keyboard, the world beyond my computer would disappear and I would be sucked into a vortex of links to a different universe. Without leaving my chair I could educate myself on the most obscure aspects of my condition and each of the choices I had to make. For hours my body barely moved. Sierra would come to my office wanting me to read Harry Potter and I wouldn't hear her. I barely spoke to Delia. If the phone rang I didn't respond. The power of having whole libraries instantly at my fingertips was like a narcotic, walling me off to the world and numbing me to the strong feelings that were lurking just under the surface.

Yet, the deeper I went, the more these questions of valve and blood and scalpel seemed like life and death choices, critical to my survival. In my search I became like the small child trying to force a round block through a square hole, pushing and shoving, hoping for some magic incantation that would rescue me. In my desperation I must have been praying for someone to say, "Yes, you've found the answer. Now you can make the *right* decision—you will survive." But there was no right answer, only the same difficult risks.

It was in this personal subterranean cave that a witchy, thin-wire voice still whispered, *Face it; you're going to die under the surgeon's knife. Drown out your fear with lousy TV, cheap novels and chocolate cookies—bury it in work, smother it in pillows each night. Whatever you do, don't feel, don't decide, don't let the full force of your fear erupt like a volcano; don't face what has to be faced.*

There were other factors also working in the sub-basement of my soul. Years ago, big decisions had been extremely difficult for me. I hadn't trusted that I could make good choices under high stake circumstances. If I made a decision that turned out badly, I would have to pay the consequences of that choice, something I tried to avoid at all costs. Big decisions reminded me that I had to step out into an unknown future where I might not succeed, where things could get very rough or I wouldn't know how to cope. I didn't like that sort of risk.

I reacted by either procrastinating for as long as possible, or by involving someone else in the decision. If the situation turned out badly, it became *their* decision not mine. I wasn't conscious of any of this—it just happened. If I had realized what I was doing, I would have been appalled. I only knew that certain decisions were slow and difficult, and that I tended to put things off. The higher the stakes, the worse it got.

Now in this new crisis, much of the old hesitancy had come back to haunt me.

CHAPTER 4

The Ghost in the Operating Room

(Waking from Obsession)

The Summer Day

Who made the world?
Who made the swan, and the black bear?
Who made the grasshopper?
This grasshopper, I mean—
the one who has flung herself out of the grass,
the one who is eating sugar out of my hand,
who is moving her jaws back and forth instead of up and down—
Now she lifts her pale forearms and thoroughly washes her face.
Now she snaps her wings open, and floats away.
I do not know exactly what a prayer is.
I do know how to pay attention, how to fall down
into the grass, how to kneel down in the grass,
how to be idle and blessed, how to stroll through the fields,
which is what I have been doing all day.
Doesn't everything die at last, and too soon?
Tell me, what is it you plan to do with your one
wild and precious life?

—Mary Oliver

Early one Saturday morning, in that dazed state between sleep and wakefulness, I was startled by a scene flashing through my mind.

I'm in the operating room standing next to the wall, watching the surgeon work on my heart. I see a ghost hovering over the table and think, *Have I died?* The ghost looks at me reproachfully. He's trying to speak but there is no sound, so I watch his lips. He mouths, "What a waste! Couldn't you have made better use of your last precious weeks doing something a little more meaningful? Stop being so obsessive!"

A few months after retirement I had begun to look at what I might do with the rest of my life. I hadn't gotten very far, but I was sure of one thing: I wanted to use my retirement years in a way that counted. So, with this dream as a reminder, I decided that I must stop obsessing and move on.

Before breakfast I took one last look at the issues. Then, with shaking hands and a silent prayer, I forced myself to make the decisions: I would have the Maze procedure, request the mechanical valve, and fully commit to the surgery date in August.

As soon as breakfast was over I took an early morning walk. I felt so much lighter, almost floating along the sidewalk that borders the beach near our house. By the time I returned, I felt a whole new energy that hadn't been there for weeks.

When I got back, I noticed some papers on my desk I had been avoiding. It was the Advance Medical Directive. Here was another reminder of how serious things were. But now I was so energized that I decided to work on it over the weekend, determined to finish it in time to sign before a notary Monday morning.

The document was in two parts: the Advance Medical Directive,[3] sometimes called a Living Will, and a Medical Power of Attorney. The Medical Power of Attorney would give my wife the legal right to make medical decisions for me. That was easy—I just had to sign it.

The Living Will was a different matter. It dealt with a whole series of decisions, all around what to do if I became massively debilitated or terminally ill, especially if I could no longer communicate my wishes. The document was designed so the patient could read it, scratch out or initial various sections and sign it with a notary. But I didn't like the choices. Instead, I tried to visualize myself in each medical situation, tried to sense what it would be like so I could be very clear about how I wanted the doctors and nurses to handle my care.

---

[3] See your local hospital, doctor, or bookstore, or search online

What should they do about pain? If I was going to die in a few days, would I want them to give me water so my body wouldn't become dehydrated, or should they stop fluids, hastening the inevitable end? At what points should they withhold CPR or other forms of resuscitation?

The most difficult decisions concerned that thin grey area between life and death. I had such a strong desire to live, was so unwilling to die, that I didn't want to make any mistake. Where was the line between continuing the struggle and letting nature take its inevitable course? At what point should I be taken off life support so my body could die in peace? I didn't want to saddle my family or my body with a long hopeless ordeal, but I did want to make sure the doctors had exhausted every reasonable possibility. My biggest fear was that even though it might appear from the outside as though I was gone, my essence or awareness, the essential 'I', might be hidden deep inside, invisible yet not wanting to depart.

All weekend I labored over the document. I had downloaded a copy from the Internet which I now modified to match my wishes. This time, besides talking it over with Delia, I called Christopher and my two other children, all living in Montana, and discussed it with them. Then, to make sure I had covered everything, I spoke with my spiritual advisor. By late Sunday night it was ready and first thing Monday morning, with Delia at my side, I signed it in front of a notary.

What a relief. Now I felt free to look for additional ways to respond to what the ghost of my dream had told me.

CHAPTER 5

The Knight and the Holy Oil

(Ritual for the Task Ahead)

The Bushman storytellers talk about two kinds of hunger.
They say there is physical hunger, then what they call
the Great Hunger.
That is the hunger for meaning.
There is only one thing that is truly insufferable,
and that is a life without meaning.
There is nothing wrong with the search for happiness.
But there is something great—
meaning—
which transfigures all.
When you have meaning you are content,
you belong.

Sir Laurens van der Post
from the documentary *Hasten Slowly*

Far away there in the sunshine are my highest aspirations.
I may not reach them, but I can look up and see their
beauty, believe in them, and try to follow where they lead.
—Louisa May Alcott

The reproach of the ghost in my dream was gnawing at me. *This is a precious time—use it wisely.*

Looking up from my morning journal entry, I was distracted by some of the objects I keep near the window: three owl feathers found on a woodland trail; pink granite pebbles, scooped dripping and cold from the bottom of my favorite spring; a conical beach shell, its brittle skin sliced open to reveal its secret heart; lava from Idaho, burned brown and porous like clinkers from the furnace my father stoked when I was five; a flake of petrified wood, chipped from a Montana tree as though cut by a woodsman's axe just yesterday.

Friends have added small gifts: a happy Buddha carved from wine-red wood; a clay Ganesh beating a shaman's drum; a wolf's features etched in polished stone; a tiny white-haired Merlin complete with blue cape, peaked cap and tall magician's staff. All these and more compete for space. On the wall behind are pictures: a portrait of Puma in his mountain lair; Isis, goddess of ancient Egypt, holding her dead husband's body; and a knight kneeling in prayer. In the center of the table is a candle that I light on special occasions, such as when a friend is battling cancer or when someone asks for my prayers. Friends call it my altar, so my altar it has become, its objects sometimes speaking to me in quiet ways.

Today, it was the knight[4]. I took the picture down from the wall for a closer look.

A young knight dressed in chain mail and red tunic is kneeling on a cushion, head bowed, steel helmet on the stone floor beside him. A beautiful young princess in a flowing white and gold gown stands facing him. Her long red hair streams in soft waves down the length of her back; her dress falls in smooth folds to the floor. In her hand is a bright sword that she has just placed on the young man's right shoulder. In the background a few people watch as solemn witnesses. It's obvious that the knight is being blessed and dedicated for some important and difficult task ahead.

When I first got the picture, I had felt both drawn yet somehow embarrassed. Even though I liked it, it felt juvenile, part of early childhood fantasies of King Arthur and his Round Table, stories I should have outgrown long ago. Despite my embarrassment, I had kept it on the wall but never explored its possibilities.

---

[4]   Edmund Blair Leighton (1853-1922)—*The Accolade*, 1901

Today, however, I could feel the picture calling to me on some deep, not yet conscious level. I picked up my journal and let words flow without thought or editing.

I love the detail. I have a crush on the young woman. I want to be a part of the picture. The knight is wearing chain mail for protection and for battle. It won't be safe where he's going. There is a powerful sense of dedication, of seriousness and clarity of purpose. Although he is going into battle, he has taken off his helmet which makes him open and vulnerable before this young woman.

The knight will face the fears, confront the dragon and battle the troll. (Or is it a spiritual journey, some sort of Grail quest[5]?) In either case, it's the princess, not the King who is anointing him with his sword. She is there for a feminine balance and to remind him to stay honest and just and to always act with integrity.

Although he may meet many others along the way, our knight's core experience will be lonely. This loneliness may be his place of weakness, the one chink in his armor that could move him off his chosen path. Drawing on his memory of this young woman (his feminine) will be a powerful force to help him with this challenge.

In my reverie, the operating room ghost had asked me to change, but it would not be easy to overcome entrenched habits. If I wanted to acknowledge what he had said, to commit to a better way to prepare for the upcoming surgery, I would need help. Perhaps I could borrow from this young knight. That evening I gave one of my friends a call.

"Mary Ann," I said. "When we get together next Friday, I would like some help. You are so good at creating meaningful ritual. I want to break out of my fear and obsession around this surgery."

"Tom, I'd be happy to help. Is there anything you would like me to bring?"

"No, just your wonderful self. Do you remember my picture of the lady and the knight?"

---

[5]   "The Holy Grail is generally considered to be the cup from which Christ drank at the Last Supper and the one used by Joseph of Arimathea to catch his blood as he hung on the cross... In the time of Arthur, the quest for the Grail was the highest spiritual pursuit."

"Sure," she said, "the one on the wall over your altar."

"Yes. I want to use that picture in whatever we do."

"Sounds good," she said. "We could knight you in the garden."

I first met Mary Ann a few years before when my friend Tala had asked Delia and me to come to a small gathering of people doing shamanic journeying.[6] I had no idea what journeying was, nor that it would play such a pivotal role in my life, but I trusted Tala and decided to go. (Later I would learn that when Tala suggests something like this and I agree, it's the prelude to an inner earthquake, a seismic shift in my inner landscape.) I remembered that first shamanic "journey" so vividly.

Delia and I are sitting with six others, including Mary Ann, in a circle in someone's living room. After chatting for a few minutes and introducing ourselves, Tala says, "It's time to start. The purpose of our first journey is to learn how to go to a place called the lower world. You will lie on the floor with something over your eyes to keep out the light. Many shamans use the rapid beat of a drum in their 'travels', so I will drum for you on this journey. Once the drum starts, use your imagination to visualize a place you know—a spring or favorite tree or hole in the ground—a place where you can descend into the earth. Continue downward until you come out somewhere. Once there, explore until you hear a change in the pattern of the drum beat. That's the callback. Retrace your steps, return to this room and open your eyes."

As soon as we're all settled comfortably, Tala starts.

For a few moments I hear nothing but the drum. Then I remember the instructions: "Go to my entry point to the lower world and descend into the earth." *This is hard. How do I do this?* For my starting point I've picked a spring near the home where I grew up. I try to see myself dive into the spring and going downward, but I can only splash around in its pool. After two or three attempts I can finally see myself descend through a dark and sloping tunnel. I reach out and touch the wall to my left, feeling the damp soil and tiny roots from the plants above. Cautiously I inch forward. *What had Tala said? "Continue until you come out somewhere—then explore?" This tunnel goes on forever. How will I get out?* Despite my hesitations, I keep going.

After what seems like hours I see a bit of light up ahead. Soon I'm at the mouth of a cave high up on a cliff. I look out into sunlight, green

---

[6]   See *The Way of the Shaman* by Michael Harner, HarperCollins, 1980, 1990

forest and distant ocean. The cliff is a sheer wall; I can't go any farther, so I back up and try again. This time there is a scree slope below me, but it's too steep and loose to climb back safely when I return. On the third attempt I come out in a pleasant wooded area and wander around until I come to a tiny swamp.

I'm enjoying the sound of swamp frogs, when suddenly the scene shifts. Now I'm in a canoe on a winding flat stream, tall reeds and marsh on either side. I paddle for a while, passing some red-wing blackbirds and a harrier hawk that's flying low looking for dinner. I come to a large patch of ripe wild cranberries and realize I am to pick them to take back to my tribe. Somehow I've become a Native American.

Again there is a slight shift. I'm crouched low, hidden behind the reeds and holding a cocked bow. In front of me, not ten yards away, is a magnificent ten-point buck who has just dipped his head for a drink. I'm to kill the buck and take him back to the tribe.

The 'me' that's lying on the floor back in the room is repulsed. I hate killing and I've never hunted. But the 'me' in the journey realizes the tribe is counting on me. We need this buck for food. So I raise my bow, let the arrow fly to its mark, killing the buck with a single shot. As I load the carcass into the canoe, I hear the change in drum beat calling me back.

After we all share our experiences Tala says, "Now we'll do a second journey to look for what's called a "power animal[7]". Descend into the earth as before. When you come out, watch to see if an animal shows up. You'll know it's a power animal if he or she appears at least four times or in four ways. Once found, hang out with them until the drum calls you back."

This time when I arrive in the same wooded glade, I see deer everywhere, dozens of them. Is my power animal a deer? This doesn't seem right. My power animal should be something big and ferocious like a bear or wolf or tiger, not a wimpy deer. But the deer persist, so finally I relent.

Now all the other deer disappear leaving only one. I walk up to him and stroke his side. As I'm standing there I feel myself slip into his body,

---

[7]   All shamanic cultures have a close relation to the natural world. For most shamans, animal spirits are important. The role of a *power animal* is to keep everyone healthy, spiritually balanced, and protected from harm. It is through these *power animals* and other teachers that shamans gain their ability to heal, to bring people's spirits into harmony, and to find answers for their community.

feel the uneven ground through all four hooves and look out at the world through his eyes.

The part of me still back in the room is amazed. Nothing like this has happened to me before. Here I am, inside a wild animal's four-legged body. I'm seeing through his eyes, hearing his sounds, experiencing his world as he does. I'm awestruck.

Back in the journey, I wander as the buck through the woods, chewing on bits of grass, sniffing the breeze and finding things to munch on. After a while I come to my harem of three doe, one of which is in heat. We mate. Thirsty from my efforts, I wander to a nearby stream and bend my head to drink. At this precise moment the hunter loosens his arrow. I feel it pierce my side and fall to my knees, dying.

I stand over the dead animal, pull out my knife and skin the carcass. Placing the meat in the canoe I wrap myself in the deer's skin. I'm feeling the very odd sensation of being both hunter and hunted, the two of us united as one.

I climb into the canoe, paddle to my tribal home and enter the dance for a successful hunt just as the drum calls me back.

*   *   *

That night was the beginning of a big change. How could this vivid experience, an experience with so much coherence and meaning, appear just from lying on the floor and listening to a drum with my eyes closed? The world view I had been able to count on since childhood—mechanistic, solid, tangible, grounded in science and technology—could not easily account for this new reality.

But I was too fascinated to stop. I soon became a serious student of shamanism and the journey process. I even trained for three years to be a part-time shamanic practitioner, helping a number of people with various spiritual issues. Over the next few years I met many more teachers and power animals, inner guides whom I slowly learned to trust. I became more attuned with plants and animals and all of nature, learning to listen for what they might tell me.

*   *   *

Through all these new explorations, my friendship with Mary Ann deepened, and after a year or so we began journeying together on a regular basis. However, today, at my request, she was coming to "knight" me in the garden as a way to help shift my attitudes about the upcoming surgery. When I saw her walking up the path, I breathed a sigh of relief. Once inside, I gave her a big hug.

"Thanks for coming."

"Oh, I wouldn't miss this for anything!" she said, as she put down her things. "This will be a nice change from our journeys."

"Have you found a statement—a vow or purpose—to go with this knighting ritual, something you aspire to?"

"Not yet," I replied as I led her to the couch. "I was waiting to talk it through with you. That always helps."

For the next few minutes we explored various possibilities. Finally I said, "Let's use, 'From this moment forward I am moving down a new path to surgery, one where I am not driven by fear but rather actively seek a healthier approach.'"

"Sounds good—let's do it."

As I stepped out into the garden to be "knighted" by Mary Ann, I began to feel silly. *This is little kid stuff, like playing dress-up. Why am I doing this?* But I knew perfectly well why I was doing it: because I was pretty sure it would help. So I kept going, fighting the urge to run back into the house and call it all off.

In the garden, so much was in bloom. The Cecile Brunner Rose was spreading a vast bank of pink blossom high into the corner maple, while at ground level the riotous colors of blue salvias and yellow and pink Peruvian Lilies were competing for our attention. To the south, the new leaves on the apple, pear and plum trees provided shade from the late spring sun.

At the edge of the back yard Mary Ann found a four-foot stick. Walking a few steps down one of the winding stone paths, we were soon in a quiet spot at the edge of the trees with roses on either side. I turned to face Mary Ann, knelt on the hard stone, and bowed my head. As I spoke the intention three times, she tapped me repeatedly on each shoulder with the stick. When we were done, we paused for a few moments, letting the full impact of the moment sink in.

"That's better already," I said. "I think this might help, but I'm also curious where this will take me."

Three days later, at 7:30 in the morning, I drove to an appointment with Cathy, my spiritual advisor. Tala had introduced me to her saying, "I have been seeing Cathy for years—you should try her." This time, I hoped to use her listening ear and supportive feedback for additional guidance.

When I told her about the knight she said, "Ritual and ceremony are time-honored ways to prepare for a difficult task. They can add a mythic dimension to your experience, a transcendent perspective that enlarges your vision beyond the narrow focus of your fears. I have a tiny vial of holy oil a priest gave me. Knights were often anointed as part of their preparations. If the idea appeals to you, you can borrow the vial."

"I'd like that."

Over the next two weeks whenever friends came, I asked them to help. Sometimes they anointed my forehead as a blessing, sometimes my hands so I would act with good intent, and sometimes my feet for the arduous road ahead. With my intention and these two rituals, I had taken another step on my quest for something better than being locked up in fear.

CHAPTER 6

Two Parables

(Help for a Paradigm Shift)

I Will Not Die an Unlived Life

I will not die an unlived life.
I will not live in fear
of falling or catching fire.
I choose to inhabit my days,
to allow my living to open me,
to make me less afraid,
more accessible;
to loosen my heart
until it becomes a wing,
a torch, a promise.
I choose to risk my significance,
to live so that which came to me as seed
goes to the next as blossom,
and that which came to me as blossom,
goes on as fruit.
—*Dawna Markova*

Having made the commitment, I continued my search. What sorts of resources or experiences could I use to move toward a more creative approach? I wanted to go into surgery with a solid spiritual, emotional and physical preparation, to face the crisis well and to keep my humanity. I didn't want to end up a whiner, grouchy and demanding.

One day I got one of those emails that make the rounds, the kind that says at the bottom, "Send me on to five of your friends and you will be guaranteed happiness forever." I almost always drag these into my desktop trashcan, but this one caught my eye.

Grandfather and the Two Wolves

Late one afternoon, just at sunset, an old Native American and his grandson were gathering wood for the evening fire. Grandfather was telling a story to the boy as they worked. "Grandson", he said, "There are two wolves buried deep inside each of us, carrying on a constant battle for our attention. One is the wolf of hatred and greed, fear and arrogance, lies and war. The second is the wolf of love and kindness, gratitude and courage, compassion and friendship." Grandfather proceeded to describe the intense struggle that went on almost daily.

The grandson listened for a while, then said, "Grandfather, which wolf is winning?"

"Ah," Grandfather replied, "The one we feed the most!"

I had put so much attention into my first wolf—a compulsive search for answers that didn't exist and focusing only on survival—that my second wolf appeared thin and gaunt, dramatically undernourished. Who was this second wolf anyway? What did he look like for me? Then almost miraculously I got some of my answer in a second email.

The Stone Cutters

Imagine a modern day reporter transported to the 12th century, to the construction site of one of the great European cathedrals. The reporter is interested in the stories of the everyday people, so he decides to interview three stone cutters, asking them what their lives are like.

The first stone cutter is busy cutting blocks of stone one foot by one foot by three quarters of a foot. In between the blows of hammer to chisel he says, "I hate this work. By the end of the day I'm exhausted and bored, doing the same damn thing over and over. It's terrible."

The second stone cutter is also busy cutting blocks of stone one foot by one foot by three quarters of a foot. "I'm happy with this work because

I can earn enough to feed my family and keep a warm, dry roof over our heads."

The third stone cutter is busy cutting blocks of stone one foot by one foot by three quarters of a foot. With an almost beatific smile he says, "I'm so blessed to be involved in the creation of a magnificent cathedral to God that will last at least a thousand years!"

The task for each stone cutter remained the same—what was different was how each viewed his life. I didn't have a choice about getting a leaking mitral valve or the need for surgery, but I could choose how I would experience that. Like the third stone cutter, there might be a way to welcome the surgery, to make it an opportunity rather than a personal disaster, even turn it into a cathedral.

As the days went by I read and reread this simple fable as a mantra for change. The stone cutters story had become a good first step in my search for the second of Grandfather's two wolves. Just by looking for him, he was becoming sleeker and better fed.

As I continued, two ideas came to me.

In order to operate on the inside of my heart, the surgical team would have to stop both my heart and my breath while they worked their magic. But in my childhood, that was how the doctor knew that the patient had died. I remembered an image from an old silent movie: The family doctor has been called to the bedside of the obscenely wealthy grandmother. While the greedy grandson stands next to the bed, an obsequious look of concern on his face, the doctor leans over and puts his ear to her chest. Hearing no heartbeat, he grimly shakes his head. Then, to make sure, he pulls a small mirror from his bag and holds it just over her mouth. Seeing no vapor of escaping breath he pronounces her dead. The grandson can no longer hide his pleasure. Fade out.

According to these childhood beliefs, I would be "dead" for a few hours, only to be returned to life at the end of the operation. Philosophers and religious people have been fascinated with this for millennia. In a couple of months, with the help of modern medicine, I would be like the phoenix, the bird from ancient Greek mythology who is destroyed in the flames of her nest every five hundred years, only to be born again out of the ashes. Could I die to old mistakes and regrets, then arise anew from the ashes of the surgery? Would this experience work me, like the smithy works the iron at the hot forge, moving me further into my humanity? While reading the Harry Potter series to Sierra, I had learned of Harry's rescue by a phoenix that lived in Dumbledore's office. Could the account of Dumbledore's phoenix help "rescue" me from my fears?

My fears had been telling me, *There's only one way to view what is happening to you and that's the narrow, tunnel-vision horror-story I tell you.* But now it seemed that these fables could open me to all sorts of possibilities. Perhaps starting down this new path toward more open vistas would bear fruit. Could I find the poet's voice that would help me interpret this crisis in a way that would empower and heal me, giving me the courage and strength I needed for the task ahead? More important, could I allow myself to be inspired? Could I open myself enough to let these stories change me, placing them deep enough in my heart so they could help? I didn't know, but just asking the questions was lifting my spirits and beginning to change my outlook.

CHAPTER 7

The Sailor

"Security is mostly a superstition. It does not exist in nature, nor do the children of men as a whole experience it. Avoiding danger is no safer in the long run than outright exposure. Life is either a daring adventure, or nothing. To keep our faces toward change and behave like free spirits in the presence of fate is strength undefeatable."

—*Helen Keller*

O f all my major decisions, only one remained: I must commit to a surgeon. Even though I had set a surgery date, I still felt highly conflicted about Dr. Valve-a-Day. During earlier web browsings, I had found a professor of cardiac surgery at a nearby university hospital. He was older, had a strong reputation as a teacher and researcher, and did about fifty valves a year. I'll call him "The Professor". Today was my appointment.

As Delia and I climbed the stairs to the cardiovascular research wing, we were greeted by warm muted colors and soft lighting. The Professor's secretary came bustling out of her office to greet us.

"Can I get you anything? Tea? Water? Coffee?"

"Just some water, thank you."

"Tea for me please."

When she returned she said, "I expect the doctor will be ready to see you in just a few minutes. Meanwhile, can I get you anything else or answer any questions?"

"No thanks."

"Fine. I'll be in my office if you need me."

After a short wait, the surgeon arrived and introduced himself with a smile and a warm handshake. As he led us to his office, I noticed how much his rotund shape and rumpled gray suit reminded me of one of Christopher's doctors at Massachusetts General Hospital in Boston. Dr. Toch had been one of the kindest, most patient of physicians, a man with a big heart and an office full of balloons for his small patients. His kindness had made a huge difference during those difficult years. Already I was feeling better.

In The Professor's office, the tables and chairs were stacked high with books and papers, reminding me of childhood visits to my Dad's genetics lab. Sitting us both in overstuffed chairs, the surgeon displayed the morning's echo results on his computer monitor. With infinite patience he showed us exactly what was happening with my heart valve and why the surgery was necessary. Using drawings and flip charts he explained in detail how the valve would be repaired and answered all my questions with a great deal of warmth and caring.

On the way back to our car, I realized that the deep visceral place inside me, the place where I had felt so uncomfortable with Dr. Valve-a-Day, felt just the opposite with this man. Yet my mind kept saying, *I know you like him, but he only does fifty valves a year while Dr. Valve-a-Day does three-hundred. Also, his reputation is not as good, and he's not so well known outside the university setting. Don't use him!*

Now I was *really* at an impasse. How was I to resolve this dilemma of gut vs. head, feelings vs. competence? I wanted to be able to trust Dr. Valve-a-Day but my feelings wouldn't let me.

Many spiritual disciplines speak of bringing our lives into harmony or balance where all the parts of ourselves are acknowledged and accepted, all parts moving toward wholeness. Much spiritual healing works because the client is helped to return to this place of inner harmony. Perhaps I could find such harmony, not by ignoring the feelings, but rather by finding a solution that could tell them, *Yes, I hear you. What you are telling me is important. I'm going to find some way to help you feel better because I want you working with me, not against me as we face this crisis.*

I decided to visit Dr. Valve-a-Day's hospital. Before going, I made some phone calls and web searches. The heart wing where I would be staying was, like the surgeon, considered the best in the region. I would be getting top medical care with highly competent doctors and nurses. If they were so good, maybe they would also pay attention to some of the subtler aspects of healing, things like helping the patient *feel* cared for during recovery.

In addition, the hospital's web site had a place for sending emails to patients. These would then be printed and hand delivered daily. I liked this. Friends and family are very important. I wanted the reassurance of their caring messages, especially from those living a long distance away who could not visit in person.

Best of all, the hospital had a place on campus for family members with special needs. Delia wanted to be with me through the surgery, but for years her driving had been limited to familiar streets close to home. A place such as this would be most welcome. And it was free.

A few days later I drove to the hospital. Wandering around the parking lot, I soon found signs to the place where Delia might stay. As I opened the weathered gate, I found myself on a winding path with green shrubbery and cool shade trees. Thirty feet ahead was a little bench for quiet contemplation. As I stepped forward, the hospital and parking lot quickly disappeared and I became surrounded by beautiful garden. In a few more paces I arrived at a pleasant home. Peering in through the glass in the front door, I saw a kitchen, common area, and a corridor that must have led to the rooms for patient family members. I didn't go in, not wanting to disturb anyone, but the ambiance was restful and welcoming.

Even the hospital was surrounded with colorful gardens and inviting shade trees. After a bit I wandered inside and took the elevator to the second floor heart wing. As I walked past one of the nursing stations, a young nurse looked up and gave me a big smile. As I smiled back I thought, *This young woman and others like her will be caring for me, not the surgeon. His magic hands will do the initial repairs, but it's the nurses who will care for me during recovery, the nurses whom I will see again and again each day. My wife and two of my best friends are nurses; and they are some of the most loving, compassionate, competent people I know. If the people watching over me while I'm here are even one tenth as nice, I will be in wonderful hands.*

On the drive home I realized that most of my feelings had been addressed. I was almost ready to fully commit my body to Dr. Valve-a-Day's skillful hands, but my feelings about him personally were still unresolved. Perhaps a shamanic journey would settle the issue.

On Friday morning Mary Ann arrived for some journey time. When it was my turn, we crafted the following purpose or "intention" for my journey: "I like Dr. Valve-a-Day's expertise. Please help me let go of the negative feelings I still have toward him so I can fully trust that he is the right surgeon for me."

I lay on the floor near my altar and put a bandana over my eyes to keep out any light. Mary Ann picked up her hand drum and began a rapid steady rhythm. I rode the sound of the drum into the shaman's world of vision and spirit.

I am standing in the mouth of a cave near the top of a high cliff. To my right a waterfall drops a thousand feet into a lush green valley. All around me are tall snow-capped peaks. I spread my wings and glide downward, heading for a familiar log circle centered in a grass-filled clearing. At the last moment, I back-peddle the air to break my descent and land at the edge of the circle. One of my lower-world teachers appears, a muscular young Native American full of grace and wisdom. I tell him why I have come and he motions me to sit with him on one of the logs.

After a few moments of quietly enjoying his presence, the scene shifts. Now, instead of sitting on a log, I'm struggling to stand upright on a wooden deck that's pitching and heaving under my feet. I feel wind-driven rain on my face and hear the creak of mast and stay. We are on a large ship under full sail, rushing headlong into a storm with hurricane winds, huge waves, and salt spray everywhere. Lightning and thunder flash and crack right next to us—the smell of ozone fills the air. A Gandalf-like figure[8], white hair and long white beard blown back by the wind, is standing in the bow. He holds a tall staff in his right hand and faces the storm with an air of determination and power. He does not calm the sea, but confidently guides the ship through the hazardous waters. His courage and strength of purpose help quiet my fears.

My teacher tells me that this is the Sailor, the one who takes long trips into the open seas and the unknown. He has the skills to maintain this aging ship, including how to stitch up any sails torn by the high winds.

I ask my teacher to let me see what is on the other side of the storm. He responds, "No, not now. This is a journey of faith and trust. You must trust that this guide and I will lead you through."

As I continue to watch, The Sailor/Galdalf figure goes through a series of rapid changes—now he looks like one of my teachers, now a power

---

[8]   Gandalf—a benevolent and powerful wizard in J.R.R. Tolkien's *Lord of the Rings* trilogy.

animal. Again and again the transformation occurs until they all appear, all my teachers and power animals united as one to help me. In one final metamorphosis he becomes Dr. Valve-a-Day, guiding my body through the storm of surgery. The 'I' on the floor in my room weeps with relief. I will not be alone.

The journey scene shifts again. We are still on the ship, but now the sea is glassy and calm. Everything is quiet. Despite the peacefulness I'm nervous. As I look around I see that we are far from the sight of land, far from the familiar, from what feels safe. As I watch I feel the sea slowly lift the boat five or six feet and then just as slowly settle it back down. I think, "Wow, there must have been an earthquake somewhere! That felt like a tsunami[9] passing under us." My teacher responds, "Yes, everything that you thought was the safe shore has been destroyed by a great tidal wave."

I hear the drum change to the "call back" signal. It's time for the journey to end.

When I returned to the room and opened my eyes, I couldn't wait to tell Mary Ann what had happened. The story poured out of me in a great river of relief. I thought, *I can do this! I can go ahead with the surgery. Although still very scary, it will be much safer to go through the unknown surgery than procrastinate on the 'safe' shore of the familiar.*

As for my uncertainty with Valve-a-Day, not only had my teacher shown me the trustworthy Gandalf, who, as the Sailor, repairs sails (valves) and guides ships through dangerous waters; but he must also have worked some additional inner change, because my old feelings of doubt no longer mattered.

That afternoon I called Valve-a-Day's office to fully commit myself to his care.

---

[9]   Note: this journey occurred more than a year before the Indian Ocean tsunami of 2004.

CHAPTER 8

Fear and the Buddhist Student

"Let me assert my firm belief that the only thing we have to fear is fear itself—nameless, unreasoning, unjustified terror which paralyzes needed efforts to convert retreat into advance."
—*Franklin D. Roosevelt,* First Inaugural Address

O ne Friday morning, after listening to my litany of fears, Mary Ann told me the following fable.

Fear and the Buddhist Student

There once was a student under the tutelage of a great Buddhist Master. One day her Master said, "It is time for you to do battle with Fear." This was a difficult request. The student was not a violent person and the thought of fighting anyone or anything seemed contrary to her nature, so she tried to argue against it. However the Master insisted, so she retired to prepare herself.

Soon it was time. With trepidation, she approached the ring and stepped through the ropes to do what must be done. As she stood up she could see in the opposite corner a huge, ugly, revolting monster that was breathing fire and shaking the very earth with his steps. It was Fear, awesome and terrifying in all his glory. Nervously she stepped forward until she was directly in front of him, her body shaking in terror. His stench was rank in her nostrils, his roar deafening. Barely able to stand her ground, she bowed low three times, asking for permission to do battle.

The monster paused in his stomping and roaring, clearly flattered by her respect.

The student asked, "Fear, please tell me—how can I defeat you?"

Fear replied, "Because you have the courage to stand here before me, I will tell you. I may appear fierce and terrifying or quiet and subtle, but whenever I am present, you will not be able to ignore me. However, even though you shake and tremble, as long as you never follow my instructions, never do what I tell you, I cannot have power over you."

Sometimes it felt as though my fears of surgery were rushing toward me like a run-a-way freight train where I couldn't step aside because I was lashed to the tracks. There was a very scared part of me that didn't want to find out what the fear was really about because then I would have to face it, feel it, and acknowledge how scared I really was. At those times I wanted to find a tiny mouse hole, crawl in, and pull the entrance in after me.

But after brooding for a while on this story, I realized that it wouldn't help to run away. I couldn't avoid the surgery, and it wasn't doing any good to bury myself in novels or TV (my equivalent of drugs or alcohol). That's what the fear was telling me to do. It also wouldn't help to ignore the fear, saying "I'm fine. I'm ready. Bring it on!" That wasn't honoring the fear. It was there. It did exist. Stuffing it under the rug would not get rid of it. If I did that, the fear would only crawl out and pounce when I least expected it, or would shove itself deep inside, then quietly gnaw away at me, rasping my innards bloody and raw with anxiety.

But now, having worked through my issues with doctor Valve-a-Day, I could see how my fears had made me paranoid. In reality, doctor Valve-a-Day was a fine surgeon and a good man, but my fears had colored everything, from how I reacted in his waiting room and during the office visit, to all those feelings of distrust and unease.

If this allegory was right, the only way to move forward would be with a clear picture of reality. Paranoia wouldn't help. What if I faced my fears head on? What if I could name the beast and not follow fear's instructions? What if I could see and understand and speak to the root source of my fears, and by doing so, perhaps dissolve them?

Part of the reality was that this surgery carried a small but measurable risk. Although ninety-five percent of patients survive, there were the other five percent. Just in case, I decided it would be better to live these next two months preparing body and soul for success, as well as living each moment as well as I could. I didn't know what form that might take, but at least it was time to try.

CHAPTER 9

Beowulf

All men should strive to learn before they die what they are running from, and to, and why.

—*James Thurber*

O ne afternoon I read an article about the work of Dr. Daniel Siegel, a Harvard-trained psychiatrist, who is interested in the physiological workings of the brain. According to the article, the "fog of fear" impacts the way our brains respond to external events, so that we react not with our logical left brain but with our emotional right brain. Under these conditions we respond to things much more nonverbally, in a way that is "neither logical nor language-based". Fear is generated by a small, primitive, almond-sized bit of the brain called the amygdala[10]. When something scary happens, the amygdala shifts into survival mode. With no time to assess the situation, no time to look at the facts, the only reaction is fight, flight or freeze. This is why it is so hard to think clearly or to make good decisions when we are fearful.

More searching revealed various medical problems that can appear when one experiences extended anxiety: things like a weakened immune system, excessive fatigue, the triggering of various auto-immune diseases, even depression. None of these seemed helpful for facing major surgery. All these thoughts reminded me of a much earlier moment of fear.

---

[10] Amygdala—a primeval arousal center, originating in early fishes, which is central to the expression of negative emotions in man.

I'm at four thousand feet, sitting in the pilot's seat of a little one-engine Cessna. The roar of the motor fills the cockpit. The rolling New England hills far below are mostly woodland and pasture, with a few houses scattered about. Three or four tiny ribbons of road wander toward the horizon only to be lost in the distant trees.

It's my fifth flying lesson and I'm gripping the yoke so hard my knuckles have turned white. Airplanes have fascinated me since childhood and I've wanted this for a long time, but the reality is such an odd mixture of wild exhilaration and gut wrenching fear. I love being up above the world, moving through three dimensional space, mastering a new skill. But my hands don't know that. Like some completely separate entity, they only know to lock themselves in a vice-like grip to the yoke while giving a secret prayer that this idiot they are attached to will get them down to solid ground safely and soon.

Suddenly there is silence—only the whisper of the wind slipping past the windows disturbs the absolute quiet. My body has gone rigid and I'm nearly peeing in my pants. From a great distance I hear my instructor say, "I've just cut your engine so watch your air speed. Dip the nose down a bit so you stay above 60 knots or the wings will stall." After another moment he says, "Now what are you going to do? We're in an extended glide with no engine—how are you going to get us out of this pickle? Do you have a soft place picked out where you can land without killing us, somewhere that's within reach of our glide? While we've been flying have you kept ahead of the plane, or just been along enjoying the scenery?"

I can't respond. My mind is so frozen that I sit mutely as the plane makes its inexorable glide toward the trees, rocks, and impossibly hard ground below.

Moments later he restarts the engine and I breathe a sigh of relief. "One of the things you must learn is to fly this airplane, not let it fly you. When you have trouble with your car you can just pull over to the side of the road and wait for a tow truck. Not so with an airplane. Here you must always be thinking ahead, always ready if something goes wrong."

Now, years later, with the engine of my body threatening to quit and my mind threatening to freeze again in terror, I realized I must deal with my fears of surgery enough to at least search for a softer landing. But how?

I like to get at the root causes of things, to figure out the source of a problem rather than treat the symptom. This attitude must have come from years of debugging software where, rather than Band-Aids scattered everywhere, the best fix is to find the exact code that doesn't work and rewrite it correctly. This requires an intimate knowledge of the software. To deal with my anxiety, I needed an intimate knowledge of my fear. Just as some cultures believe that if you know someone's true or spiritual name you can have power over them, I wanted to know the exact name of each fear as a first step toward conquering it. Or, to put it another way, if I could understand what I was running from and why, I might have a chance to do something about it. I also understood that I could use the fear as a powerful motivator, encouraging me to shift priorities and do things that I might otherwise ignore.

I started my inquiry with meandering walks and journal writing, first creating a simple list of almost random possibilities, hoping that the important fears would present themselves as I progressed. I thought of pain, of debilitation and stroke, of the surgeon's knife and of dying. With each possibility I wrote whatever came to me, examining how I felt and looking at any old memories that floated to the surface. I wasn't writing for style, just letting thoughts flow from the pen to see what would appear.[11]

As I continued I soon realized that I was confusing various uses of the word 'fear'. Sometimes I would be saying, "I'm afraid that X might happen." meaning "I don't want X to happen." Although important, this was not the kind of fear I was looking for. I was also confusing things I *might* be afraid of with fears that specifically applied to *me* in *this* crisis. For example, when I explored my relationship to pain, I remembered that I had a pretty high tolerance for it. Ever since childhood I had hated the aftereffects of Novocain; instead, I had always refused it, letting the dentist just drill. I had found that the discomfort lasted for only a few moments and then stopped the second the drilling stopped. This seemed much better than the hours of numbness and disturbing sensations caused by the Novocain.

Using my journal and talking to friends I eliminated such things as fear of pain, loss of abilities, and stroke. I didn't want them to happen, but they weren't the source of my particular anxiety. Instead, I soon realized that my specific enemy would be much closer to a heart-stopping, adrenalin-rushing fear: the kind that either overwhelms everything, or that forces

---

[11] See *The Artist's Way, a Spiritual Path to Higher Creativity*, by Julia Cameron. 1992

the inner self to erect thick walls of protection, hiding the fear so deep we are seldom, if ever, aware of it.

One afternoon, again doodling in my journal, I thought I would explore the surgery. My plan had been to use my imagination to climb onto a gurney, be wheeled into the operating room, and watch all the surgery steps until they finally wheeled me into intensive care some hours later. But when I started, I couldn't even get through the operating-room door! The thought of anyone taking a knife or scalpel and cutting me was terrifying. If this was one of the big fears, and I was pretty sure it was, I was going to need some help!

On a walk the next day, I was reminded of a book I had devoured the first year of retirement, David Whyte's "The Heart Aroused, Poetry and the Preservation of the Soul in Corporate America." Whyte spends a long chapter using the Anglo Saxon epic poem Beowulf[12] as a metaphor for addressing dark and difficult issues within ourselves. Here is my own summary of the part of the poem that I thought might help.

Summary of the epic poem "Beowulf"

Hrothgar, King of Denmark, has been plagued by a monster named Grendel. Night after night Grendel enters the King's hall, battles his knights, then drags his kill back to his home in a nearby swampy lake. Beowulf, a warrior prince, offers his services to Hrothgar, persuading the king to let him be his champion. The first night Beowulf and his men engage Grendel in battle, mortally wounding the monster who then hauls himself back to the lake to die.

The next day there is great celebration and feasting. But late that night a new monster, far more dangerous than the first, appears and again drags many bodies off to the lake. This is Grendel's mother, come to avenge her offspring.

This time Beowulf must descend into the dark lake to confront Grendel's mother directly. The lake is so swampy and hideous that no-one and no creature will go there and none of his men will join him. In preparation Beowulf is given a special sword and helmet and wears a protective suit of ring mail. The sword and helmet give him courage to jump in, but they become useless once he sinks to the bottom. Beowulf is forced to wrestle

---

[12]   Probably written sometime between 700 and 1000 AD.

with Grendel's Mother in hand to hand combat. In the ensuing struggles they enter her den where Beowulf sees another great sword fastened to the wall. Taking it down, he beheads the monster and returns, carrying both sword and head to the surface. On the way up however, the great sword dissolves so it could not be taken out of the swamp.

The King is pleased and hosts a great celebration where Beowulf is honored in song and story.

*   *   *

I decided to use Beowulf's descent into the lake as an inspiration for my own descent into my darkest fears.

CHAPTER 10

An Ancient Sword and the First Descent

The gift of grace can come in strange and unexpected ways. Sometimes it comes gently, like an old memory from childhood, a poem, words from a friend, or a pre-dawn dream. But sometimes it comes disguised as living nightmare. That's when the Great Smithy grabs you by the collar, drags you to his forge, and drops you into the burning coals. Then, while one mighty hand pumps the bellows to bring the flames to a white heat, the other hammers the glowing iron of your soul into some new and unexpected shape.

—*Tom Snell*

The first weapon at my disposal was like an ancient sword from the past, one that would work deep in the lake where my monster lay. Thirty years ago this weapon had been forged in the fires of that earlier crisis when Christopher had been so ill. With the dreadful prospect of heart surgery looming before me, I began to go back again and again to that period of the mid-seventies, reliving it afresh and drawing upon what I had learned. Little did I know when I started what an important resource that time in my life would be.

* * *

The year before Christopher's illness, my first wife Julie and I had bought an acre lot from The Meeting School, a small Quaker boarding school in southern New Hampshire where we were teachers and house parents. That spring we started building our house, doing everything ourselves, with the help of two college students working for summer room and board. By early December of that year we had erected the outer shell, put double plastic where the windows were to go, and added insulation. Designed for open space and energy conservation, the south living room wall would eventually yawn a full two and one half stories of insulated glass that would inhale the warmth of the winter sun. From the upstairs hallway, only a railing separated the viewer from this large open space. Toward the viewer's left was our bedroom, hanging suspended like a child's tree-house over the dining room, while hidden below were the bathroom and kitchen. A smaller wing, planned for a year or two later, would hold additional bedrooms for our children. But at this point in the construction there weren't even rooms—only open studs to mark where the interior walls would eventually materialize.

All of us, Julie and I and our three young children, Christopher, Tamara, and Sarah, had been living since spring in a small summer cabin on a nearby lake. It had a tiny wood stove to combat the evening chill, but was not designed to handle New Hampshire winters. Now, with the December cold forcing us out, we moved into our new home. Julie was eight months pregnant with our fourth child, Timothy, but we had no other choice. Living was primitive. A large blanket pinned to ceiling rafters afforded the only bathroom privacy. At bedtime, we would climb a rickety aluminum ladder to our make-believe bedrooms. At least the space had heat and basic plumbing.

The intense winter cold forced all our building efforts indoors. We spent more time cleaning than working, bringing construction to a crawl. By now, not only had Timothy been born, but construction had slowed even more with the discovery that Christopher was starting puberty at seven. It took three months of weekly trips to Mass General before they finally found the rare tumor causing it. Then, over the next two years, with two operations, radiation treatment, and chemotherapy, Julie and I practically lived on the sixty-five mile route to Boston, all while trying to raise our kids, teach full time, and nurse a very sick child. All this in the mess and chaos of a very unfinished house.

One morning just after breakfast, I strapped on my tool belt to start the day's carpentry. As I pulled the tarp off the table saw that stood in the middle of our living room, something inside me snapped. When my two assistants arrived, I saw Jim open his mouth to say something, but I couldn't make out the words. Everything was distorted as though his voice was being forced through a long twisted pipe that wound its way many times around the room before finding its way to my ear. I glanced from David to Jim and back again. I looked at the table saw and felt the weight of the loaded tool belt cutting into the top of my hip bone.

"What?" I said.

Faintly, as though at a great distance, I heard, "Tom, what's the project for today?"

"This is weird," I said, sitting at the dining room table. "I know we were planning to work today, and that we have at least a dozen projects to do, but I can't think of a single one."

"So, what do you want us to do?" asked David, sitting beside me, a look of concern on his face.

"I don't know. Maybe we should all take the day off," I said with a shrug.

"OK, but take care of yourself," Jim said, as they started out the door. "We'll check in with you tomorrow and see how you are."

For the next few days I wandered around the house like a zombie. Something was wrong and none of us liked it.

Four days later Julie stalked into the bedroom where I had been napping and confronted me. "Tom, this is too much! You've got to deal with this. It's affecting your work and the children." She started to pace, her voice rising louder and louder. "I can't take care of everything all by myself. The kids need you. I need you. You've got to get some help!"

"Go away," I moaned.

"No, I won't. I want you to try that co-counseling thing again that Dottie's been talking about."

"Calm down, Julie. You'll upset the kids," I said, as I propped myself up on one elbow. "Look, I tried it once and nothing happened. Remember? All I got out of that day was a splitting headache."

"Yes, Tom," she said, running her hand through her hair in frustration. "The thing is, you never get headaches. Never! That's why I think something inside you is trying very hard to break free. Go get some help, damn it! Dottie said there's going to be a big workshop in Boston in February. I want you to go."

"Well, I don't like the idea, but I'll think about it." With that, I rolled back toward the wall, and she stalked out of the room, fuming.

Over the next few days things got worse. Rather than think about it, I lay about, trying to bury everything under huge pillows of sleep. I ignored Julie and shrugging off my children whenever they needed me.

Despite all this avoidance, I had learned that the workshop was to be led by Harvey Jackins, the founder and discoverer of Co-counseling, and that it would be for eight days. But I had never been to a workshop—I didn't even know what a workshop was. The very idea of going sent shivers up my spine.

Even worse, the thought of therapy terrified me. It must have been during my childhood that therapy became equated with madness, or at least family dishonor. Any time I thought about therapy, an image would flash through my mind of big burly men forcing me into a straight jacket and hauling me away to a mental institution.

For a week I experienced an internal war between the irrational fear of possible insanity and the pressure to do something, anything, to break out of my paralysis. I kept putting it off, but finally mailed an application at the last minute. I was half hoping I wouldn't get in. Perhaps they would reject me because I hadn't fulfilled the requirement of sixteen weeks of classes. But a week later I got a letter saying I was accepted.

So one evening in February I found myself in Boston with about fifty other people, listening to the first lecture. I had chosen the seat closest to the door for my emergency escape route. I was so nervous that first night that I was constantly running to the men's room to pee.

The next morning, we divided into groups of three to practice what we had learned. This was to be half an hour each, so my two partners and I wandered off to one of the available hotel rooms. With a coach to help me, I was the first to play the role of "counselor". The woman playing "client" said, "I'm here to do some pretty deep work and I feel safest when I'm being held. Would you hold me please?"

Not knowing what that meant, I said "Sure."

The next thing I knew, she was sitting in my lap, her head on my chest and holding on like she would never let go. I wanted to do this right, whatever 'this' was, so I tried desperately to be calm. But my hands were shaking and I felt a cold sweat begin to dampen my shirt.

Luckily my coach sat right behind me. In a reassuring whisper she said, "Just put your arms around her and hold her gently. Don't say anything, just hold her." Her quiet voice began to settle my nerves and I slowly put my arms around the woman in my lap. The moment my hands and arms touched her she started to cry.

At first she cried silently but soon she was wailing. My coach kept saying, "Just hold her gently and lovingly. Everything's going exactly as it should." Meanwhile, part of me wanted to rush out of the hotel, leap into my car, and drive the sixty-five miles home, never to return. But I had paid a very precious two hundred dollars to do this workshop, so I forced myself to stay.

Suddenly the woman in my lap stopped as quickly as she had started and gave me a warm smile. Despite myself, I smiled back. I couldn't have put words to it then, but in that moment, the rigid armor I had worn since childhood began to soften ever so slightly. I let out a big sigh and could feel the worst of the tension drain from my body. As I relaxed, the woman in my arms put her head back on my chest and began again. Between sobs she started telling about a terrifying event in her childhood.

When she was six, her favorite place to play had been a quiet hide-a-way under a dense fir tree in a small patch of woods behind the family's house. That afternoon, as she played quietly, she heard two men come crashing through the underbrush. Startled and scared, she crawled behind her tree. Peeping out, she saw one man beating a smaller man with a big stick, continuing to hit him again and again long after he stopped moving. Finally the big man dropped the stick and ran away. For what seemed like forever, the little girl lay behind the tree, too terrified to move. Finally, she heard her mother calling and ran home.

As the story proceeded, the woman in my lap started to shake as well as cry. Soon she was shaking so hard I could feel her body vibrating violently against mine, and my shirt front became soaked with her tears. At the same time my coach kept murmuring, "Just hold her and remember to breathe. She's pretty experienced, so she knows just what to do."

When the story ended she started again. Again and again she told the story, sobbing and shaking and sweating through each iteration. With each telling she seemed stronger, less afraid. Finally the timer chimed, marking the end of her session. After two minutes of answering questions and looking around the room, exercises to bring her fully back to the present, she climbed off my lap. Moving to a chair opposite me, she appeared relaxed, almost radiant. Giving me a big smile, she said, "Now it's your turn."

I thought, *Amazing, look at her! Maybe this actually works. If she can do this, so can I.* Then she took both my hands in hers and said, "Just talk about anything you want to talk about."

I started to tell about my family and the house we were building. For the first few minutes it all seemed very mundane, but then something happened. To this day I don't know how it started, but the next thing I knew, I was laughing harder than I could ever remember. The laughter went on and on, seemingly endless. After some initial surprise, it began to feel liberating. Once, as I caught my breath, I noticed I was grinning, the first pleasurable smile in more than a year. In between being doubled over, holding my sides and roaring, I thought, *This is wonderful—I've got to learn how to get more of this!*

For the rest of the workshop I waited eagerly for these times when we would pair up and I could take my turn. I knew that crying and shaking were also encouraged, but I couldn't seem to do either one. For those eight days, however, the laughter was enough.

When the workshop ended, I said my goodbyes and drove home. As I walked in the house Julie gave me the strangest look.

"What's wrong?" I asked.

"You look so different!"

"What do you mean?"

"You've changed—you're standing straighter, and you're actually smiling."

"That's good. I feel much better, but I didn't realize others could see it."

"Yes, I like this new you!"

I was hooked. Soon I was commuting weekly to Boston for classes, and later Julie joined me. The two of us began traveling to workshops whenever we could afford the time and expense. Although I could often feel tears lurking just below the surface, it would be more than a year of hard work before I became free enough to cry. Meanwhile, things at home were slowly improving. I spent more time with our children. Now we encouraged their tears rather than shushing them, all to good effect. One example stood out.

With so much of our attention going to Christopher's illness, four-year-old Sarah had begun to cling. Every time Julie and I tried to leave the house, she would sit on my foot, wrap herself around my leg and refuse to let go. One evening, instead of prying her free, handing her to the babysitter, and dashing out the door, I picked her up and held her, her little arms around my neck. She immediately began to cry. Still holding her, I sat in a nearby chair and waited patiently. After ten minutes her crying began to subside. Ever so gently I reached behind my neck, took hold of her arms as though to pry them loose, and said, "Sarah, we're going now." Her response was to cry all the louder. Each time her crying slackened I would touch her arms, say, "We're going," and each time the tears would return. Finally, after half an hour, she leaned back, gave me a big smile, jumped off my lap, and ran over to the baby sitter. As we left for the evening I said to Julie, "That worked better than I hoped."

"Yes, but we should be prepared for it again the next time we leave."

A week later I again unwrapped her from my leg and held her. Once more she cried, but only for five minutes before running off to play with her toys. That was it—never again did she feel the need to cling.

Things were looking up. Little did we know that within a year, by 1974-75, we would be facing a crisis that would dwarf everything.

* * *

Now, however, in 2003, I had my own surgery to face and a huge fear of the surgeon's scalpel, so the next morning I called my fellow co-counselor Janet to set up an appointment. Janet is a warm, intelligent, loving friend with whom I exchange regular sessions. Each week I listen to her for half an hour, then she listens to me. We're very relaxed around each other's feelings, whether of fear, grief, or embarrassment, and we have learned to listen well without interruption and with much caring. Our friendship is limited to this one hour, but within those constraints we have developed a great deal of mutual safety. We can share anything, knowing that it is all held in the utmost confidence.

The next day during my turn, I talked briefly about my difficulties. "The whole thing's pretty scary. I especially hate the idea of the surgeon cutting into me."

"Okay," Janet said. "Let's try something. Lie on your back on the couch—pretend it's the operating table. I'll sit here next to you. Good! Now tell me about the surgery."

As I began to speak, she reached into her purse and pulled out an imaginary scalpel. Then, looking at me with a twinkle in her eye, she pantomimed checking the scalpel's sharpness by drawing her thumb across its edge.

Wooow, I thought, *here we go*, and immediately began to shake. Soon the whole couch was shaking with me. Within minutes I was sweating as well. The day had been chilly, so I had worn two layers. I sat up for a moment, stripped off my heavy flannel shirt, then lay back down again. Still I was hot. Slowly, as the minutes went by, the shaking and sweating lessened, so my co-counselor, clearly concerned that her scalpel was not sharp enough, began to stroke it against a pretend leather strop. Back and forth, back and forth, turning the blade just so at the end of each stroke, she perfectly pantomimed my childhood barber preparing his blade for shaving the back of my neck.

I began to giggle—she looked so ridiculous with her weak attempts at an evil grin, and the equally ridiculous leather strop. Soon I was laughing so hard my sides ached. Finally, after thirty minutes, it was over. I was exhausted but elated.

"Thanks," I said, "That was perfect."

This was much better, but I still hadn't reached my goal of going through the surgery steps. So, later that afternoon, I put on my drum CD, lay on the carpet with a cloth over my eyes, and started a descent into the lower world. Down, down, down I went, tunneling deep into the earth . . .

I'm in tall grass. It grows high so I can't see very far ahead, but I push forward. Soon I arrive at the familiar log circle. This time a White Tailed Hawk is waiting. I climb on her back. She flies up and hovers over a gigantic water filled cauldron. As I look down into the water's reflection, I see my naked body lying, face up, on a long narrow table or altar. The table is just wide enough to support my body but not my arms. These are stretched out, cross-like, straight to either side, their weight dragging my wrists and hands low toward the floor. An invisible force pulls at the center of my chest, raising my body up into the air. I'm feeling very exposed and vulnerable.

As though reading my mind, the hawk says, "Trust—it's all about trust." Then, as we watch, I am taken through all the surgery steps, seeing each stage in full detail. Nothing is left out. I watch the surgeon lift his scalpel for the first time, watch them saw through the length of my sternum, then split my chest down the center and spread it wide. I watch as they attach the heart-lung machine to my blood vessels, still my beating organ and stop my breath. Next they expose the inner workings of my heart, gaining access to the valve where the problem lies. With the most delicate tools, they snip out the damaged tissue and begin their repairs, stitching the torn leaflets to form the perfect valve it once was. After performing a single bypass using an artery from my chest wall, they close my heart and stimulate it to beat again. Next they restart my breathing and remove the heart-lung machine. Finally they restore my chest to its normal shape, close everything up and bring me back to life. As I pass successfully through each step, my body lying on the floor in my room heaves great sighs of relief and banished fear.

The hawk says, "You have just been shown the miracle of the modern operating room. Not so long ago, few of these techniques were available. Nearly everything you have seen has been developed in the past fifty or sixty years, unavailable to those who came before you. These are powerful new tools. Trust them and use them well."

As the journey came to a close I noticed that I had been crying, my face wet with tears. Yet I was jubilant! I had managed to bring my first big fear to its knees. Now it was time to look for the others that I knew were still there.

CHAPTER 11

The Hunt for Beowulf's Courage

Winning does not tempt that man.
This is how he grows: by being defeated, decisively
by constantly greater beings.

> From The Man Watching
> —*Rainer Maria Rilke*
> —*Trans: Robert Bly*

T he next day, in my musings during my morning walk on the beach, I was again reminiscing about Christopher's painful struggles with chemotherapy and how tough it had been for all of us. Christopher had survived that early ordeal and was now in his late thirties, but there was a second nightmare that had come right on the heels of the first. Despite some hesitation, I decided to revisit it.

* * *

I'm sitting in a big overstuffed sofa and gazing out a picture window at a magnificent range of snow-capped mountains. To my left is a huge fireplace with a spark shield sculpted by the local blacksmith. At night, with the shield silhouetted against the fire, half a dozen iron cowboys rise from the flames like ghostly silhouettes and herd their cows in silence across the screen. To my right, in front of a wall of books, sits a black Steinway grand, its polished surface gleaming in the light from the big picture window.

It's 1977 and I'm in the home of Julie's parents in Montana. The week before, with The Meeting School closed for the summer, we had piled our children into our old Dodge van and driven the 2,300 miles from New Hampshire for a month of respite. Now we're waiting patiently while our friend Tom Weidlinger (TW) sets up his tape recorder. TW had become fascinated with film while a student of mine at The Meeting School. Now that he's graduated, he's moved on to director's school in Los Angeles and has come to interview us as the basis of a script for a class project.

As Julie walks in from the kitchen carrying three mugs she says, "I think the kids are pretty well set for a while."

"Where are they?" I ask.

"Sarah's in the kitchen making cookies with Mother, and Tamara's gone with some carrots to try to entice that colt again. You should see her, TW. She's so into the horses this year—spends every spare minute with the ones out in the summer pasture."

"Is Chris down by the barns with the ranch mechanic?" I ask.

"Yeah," says Julie, as she drops onto the couch beside me. "He won't stop pestering the guy. He's really gotten into mechanic stuff this year—engines and tools and things."

"Thank goodness," I say, taking her hand. "It's a whole lot better than lying around the house all the time, the way he did last year."

"So, TW, are we ready to start?"

"Sure." After handing us the mike he says, "Here we go. I'm starting the tape . . . So take me back to November of 1973. What happened?"

Tom (the author) speaking:

Well, TW, you know the basic story, but we'll lay out the details for the tape.

When our youngest child, Timmy, was still three, he began running a strange fever that lasted for two weeks. The fever was the only symptom. Having gone through so much with Christopher's cancer when he was eight and nine, we were worried, so we checked our Doctor Spock book. It said, if your kid isn't really sick, don't panic, but we weren't so sure.

Julie speaking while squeezing my hand:

Yeah. I got really concerned, so one afternoon I laid him down beside Sarah and felt both their stomachs—it was then that I noticed a big bulge in his tummy. I said, "Wow, this isn't normal!" So I called the pediatrician and scheduled him for the next afternoon.

In the school's morning collection[14] I stood up and said, "Tim's been running a really weird fever and I'm taking him to the doctor today. Maybe I'm just a crazy mom, but after what I've gone through with Christopher I'm really scared," and I started to cry. After collection, everyone gathered around the two of us in a big show of love and support and promised to hold us in their prayers.

At the doctor's he felt Tim's tummy and said, "Yeah, this is really strange." Then he scheduled him immediately for blood work and X-ray. While Tim and I were waiting for the results, I got a call on the receptionist's phone.

Tom:

Yeah, it was from me.

Julie:

You were in such a twit.

Tom:

I was really upset—practically shouting into the phone. "What's going on? Mass General[15] called me. What's the matter? What did the doctor say?"

Julie:

"Well, I don't know what the doctor said. I haven't seen him yet. What's this about Mass General?" I thought, *this is really a crisis, it's really terrible, something terrible is the matter with Tim.* (Putting her head on my shoulder and crying)

So there I am in the doctor's office having this incredible conversation with Tom on a very public phone. For everyone there, it was immediately apparent that we were in crisis. In that small country clinic, they were not used to handling these kinds of crises. It's usually checkups and well-baby care. You know how you get pulled into something like that—like some huge traffic accident. All I wanted to do was scream and cry, but I couldn't because there was a wall of faces: the receptionist, the nurses and parents, all staring at me.

Tom:

The whole thing was so freaky. Why was Mass General calling? Chris didn't need admitting—his treatments were over. The people I had been

---

[14] A twenty minute gathering before school began for a brief silence and announcements.

[15] Massachusetts General Hospital in Boston, Massachusetts.

talking to were administrative staff. They knew nothing—only that they were to schedule a room and needed our insurance information. It was all like a very bad dream. (Getting louder) I wanted to yell and pound the wall.

Julie, squeezing my hand to quiet me:

What we realized later . . . After looking at the X-rays, the pediatrician had immediately conferred with Mass General. They decided we should take Tim there for further tests. Mass General had responded so quickly that Tom had gotten the hospital's call before our local doctor had a chance to hang up, finish his notes, and come out of his office to inform me.

Anyway, after we settled down a little, Tom and I talked about the arrangements of taking Tim down the next day, getting a sitter for the other kids, what we were going to do about our classes and who was going to take care of the house while we were gone, all that kind of thing. And asking people in the community to pray for us.

Finally I hung up and went out into the waiting room with Timmy. It was so unreal. Here were all these other mothers. They had been admiring each others' kids, talking about school, what teacher does she have, what does your husband do—finding those little things that connect their lives to each other. I thought, maybe if I concentrate really hard on play-acting, on being an ordinary normal mother in a doctor's waiting room, asking all these dumb questions, carrying on these inane conversations, maybe I won't have to cry. But finally it was time to leave. So I picked Tim up and, as we walked through all those mothers staring at us, I did cry. I cried all the way out. I figured, "Shit, I can't help it; it's okay if they know that something awful is happening to us."

TW:

What happened on that first trip to Mass General?

Tom:

The day we took him down, they put him through a whole bunch of tests, and half way through the day they knew what he had. "Timothy has a Whelms Tumor, a type of kidney tumor. We'll operate on him on Monday." These were doctors who already knew us through Christopher, so they knew how to approach us, and they knew that being direct was the best way. They said "It's a malignant tumor, but it's very weird. It can grow very fast or it can be unpredictable. Like a forest fire, it may stop and smolder for a long time, or the wind will change, or it will burn itself out and be fine, or it can be absolutely devastating. This one is worth the fight, even though it has already spread to his lungs."

TW:

How did you handle the tests and treatments with Timothy? Was it any different from what happened with Christopher?

Julie:

With Chris, neither of us knew how to help him with his anxiety.

Tom:

Or with our own.

Julie:

Yes. For example, the first time Chris was in the hospital I ran a temperature of 104° and was sicker than a dog. It was very clear to me, even when it was happening, that it was an emotional thing, that I couldn't handle the emotional experience. It knocked me off my feet. With Chris, I was so tight I practically went the whole summer without eating or sleeping or crying. It meant that when I sat beside his bed, that was all I could do. I wasn't really there. We would sit in the same room pretty much not talking to each other, both of us trying not to cry. I held his hand sometimes, but when that made me feel like crying, I would take my hand away. When he had to go through a scary medical procedure, I couldn't be there for him or intervene because all this emotion was blocking me.

But by the time Timothy's cancer appeared, I had learned that if I didn't start crying from the very beginning and accepting other people's help, that the same thing would happen again. I was so determined to be there for him. I knew that in order to do that, I had to take care of myself. With Timothy, I never lost a night's sleep because I cried myself to sleep every night. I never lost my appetite. I just didn't get that tight feeling. This gave me so much more inner strength to deal with the doctors and to help Tim.

TW:

Talk to me about situations where you might have intervened.

Tom:

Sometimes the nurses were not kind or thoughtful, or they had problems of their own, and they would be brusque. For example, right after his surgery, turning Chris in bed was very painful for him. If the nurse was in a hurry, she would come in and turn him quickly, just to get it over with, rather than be gentle and do it at a pace that gave Chris some control over his situation.

With Timothy, however, we would insist that they wait until he was ready. If they had been short with him in any way, we made sure that we stayed with him until he was comfortable and confident again. For example, for a four-year-old, a simple finger prick could be a big deal. I would say, "All right Timothy. You can cry and fuss all you want, but this is something that has to be done. You tell us when you're ready." But that meant that Julie or I had to hold the technician off, we had to make her wait and respond to Tim as a human being rather than let her quickly process him along with a million other people that day.

TW:

How would you hold them off?

Tom:

You tell him, Julie. You were better at this than I was.

Julie:

Well, when I was doing it I would say, very calmly, "You're not going to touch him until he's ready. I know you're busy, and I know you have a lot of people to do, but he just needs to have you give him a little space. He's dealing with a really hard experience and is doing the best he can. He's only four years old, and you're going to have to wait until he is ready." But that took a lot of presence for me to be able to confront the medical personnel that way. I didn't have that with Christopher. With Chris they tended to bulldoze all of us.

TW:

Tell me more about the differences between Chris' experience and Timothy's.

Julie:

Because we didn't intervene for Chris, didn't hold him in times of pain and crisis, it was as though he became a victim of the medical world. Essentially he was powerless: he had no say over his body, his destiny, or his well-being. In the hospital, people would come into his room at any time of the day or night and inflict any kind of misery, terror or pain, and he had no say about it. That kind of powerlessness is devastating, especially to a child. If you ever experience it yourself, even a little bit, you just know how devastating a feeling it is. After his two surgeries, every single time he had a chemotherapy infusion, which was once a week for two years, all his anxiety, fear and rage came roaring out and it would take three or four people to hold him down. He's bearing those marks right now, by the way he withdraws.

Tom:

You see, it wasn't until after all Chris' treatments were over and he was on the way to a complete physical recovery that we acquired the skills to help deal with all the feelings, both ours and Chris'.

Julie:

Yes. With Timothy, when either of our co-counselors arrived, we would find a free bedroom, close the door for half an hour, and yell and scream and cry till we were hoarse and had used up half a box of tissue. It was liberating!

Tom:

Yeah. So now, with Tim, we were so calm he didn't pick up on most of our fears and therefore wasn't making them his own. And by being present to his feelings, he didn't stay stuck in them. The difference was like night and day. Chris' fears just built and built until they were an impossible nightmare for him. Tim simply cried a little and then was done, immediately returning to his cheerful, playful four-year-old self.

At the same time, TW, even though I didn't know it then, I was being healed. Now I could hold my son when he needed me. How wonderful that felt: to hold him close, feel his warm little body next to mine, feel him relax from the initial tension of his fears, feel his trust, and find redemption by doing for Tim what I had not been able to do for Chris.

I'm not sure if, as a general rule, parents were allowed to sit with their children in the Intensive Care Unit (ICU) at Mass General. Tim's operations would take all day so he would spend at least the night in the ICU. I remember feeling so blessed that we were allowed, one at a time, to sit with him through the night. We never saw other parents there so perhaps we were an exception. Of course, by this time the doctors knew us well, knew that we could remain calm and peaceful, and not disturb Tim or the other patients, and leave immediately if they asked us to. Although Tim would be asleep nearly the whole time, I'm convinced that our calm presence helped him heal quickly and bounce back almost overnight to his lively little-boy self.

TW:

Could you give me some more details about how Timothy was handling things?

Tom:

Julie, tell about Tim's fourth big surgery. That's a good example.

Julie:

Okay.

We had driven down to Boston for one of Tim's monthly progress checks. I knew that something awful was happening because his chemotherapist was avoiding us.

Doctor Toch is a marvelous doctor from Vienna, older, about 65, with a shock of gray hair. What you might imagine a big portly Doctor Freud would look like. He had a black vest and a gold watch-chain across his broad stomach and a twinkle in his eye. He loved kids, always giving them balloons instead of candy. On each visit Tim would con him out of about ten balloons. He was the kind of doctor who it was very easy for little kids to con, because he just loved them to pieces. If the X-rays were good he would come out immediately and be radiant. In his heavy Austrian accent he would say, "I have marvelous news for you Mrs. Snell. The X-rays are excellent!"

But this time he walked by me with his head down and his brows together, and headed out into the hall. A few moments later I saw Tim's surgeon, Doctor Kim, disappear down the hall and a moment after that Doctor Linggood, Tim's radiation specialist, went by. When all three of them got together like that, I knew it was really critical. I knew it meant another operation, this time Tim's fourth.

Finally, after a long wait, they sent in Doctor Kim. He took one look at me and said, "Well, there's one mother we don't have to tell," and I burst into tears. Then he got down on his knees to talk to Tim. He said something like, "Well, old man, I have bad news for you. You have to come back and pay us another visit on Monday."

Tim looked at him and just grinned, just looked radiant. "I know," he said very brightly, and kept playing with his cars.

Doctor Kim looked at me, then at Tom, then at everyone else. I could hear Dr. Kim say to himself, "Well, this kid doesn't understand. I'll try again." So he said, "Tim, do you know why you're going to have to come in?"

Tim said, "Yup! Going to have another operation!" again very brightly. Then Kim said something else which I didn't catch, and Tim got disgusted with him, looked him straight in the eye and said, "Well, I like your hospital!"

There was nothing any of the rest of us could say. All of us grownups sat there with our mouths hanging open. I had to say, "You know, Dr Kim, he really means it. He had an operation just two months ago and two others before that. He knows exactly what's going to happen. He knows exactly what to expect, and he has that much confidence in you. He's not a bit anxious."

You know, TW, my greatest fear for my children would be to see them disintegrate as individuals. If their lives were to become such a drag, such a terror, such a pain and burden for them—like being in a concentration camp—that they would break. That's where prayer . . . I really feel that prayer and support got us healed. He was so whole, and so without anxiety about things that were happening to him.

Tom:

Yes. All sorts of people from coast to coast were praying for us.

TW:

So what happened next?

Tom:

Well, the difference between his first and fourth surgeries was like night and day. In the first, he was crying and carrying on . . . It was so hard to watch him be wheeled through the operating room door. We walked with him as far as they would let us, one on each side of the gurney, holding his hands and trying not to cry ourselves—putting on a brave front—trying to smile . . .

But in the fourth operation, he was in complete command. He sat up on the gurney with his little stuffed animal under one arm, waved a cheery goodbye, and laughed! He had a sheet around him and his baseball hat was on crooked, covering his bald head.

Julie:

Yeah, by this time he looked like a Biafran child, but with a big grin and that silly stuffed animal.

Tom:

Well, we had gone into town for the eight hours of the operation. When we got back, Tim's floor nurses crowded around to tell us what happened. The operating room nurses had come up to the children's wing to tell them how amazing Tim had been. When he got to the OR, instead of being the usual scared little kid, he was completely in charge. He was so silly. He took whatever anyone said and made a little-kid joke out of it. Soon he had the whole OR laughing. Like, when the doctor asked him to count from 1 to 10, he teased them by counting backwards instead. When he got down to eight, he opened one eye, looked up at the doctor with a mischievous grin, trying to gauge his reaction, then giggled. He was so alert, so alive and relaxed, so completely trusting of those people.

Then one of the floor nurses said, "This was so unusual. The OR nurses *always* stay down in surgery. They've *never* come up the three flights to the children's ward until now."

TW:

Thanks, both of you. You're sharing some wonderful material for my script. But I'm running out of tape, so let's break for lunch.

*   *   *

Pondering these ancient memories had carried me a long distance down the beach in my morning walk, well past the usual summer crowds. Here there were only two fisherman casting their lines into the surf, while half a dozen pelicans could be seen diving for a late breakfast just outside the breakers. On this quiet stretch of sand, I paused to examine these recollections. Chris and Tim's experiences so clearly summed up my fear and my desire—the first, so isolated and scared he has to be held down for each treatment; the second, so confident and relaxed he had the whole operating room enthralled. I thought, when it comes time for my August surgery, I want to do for myself what we did for Timothy. If I can follow his lead and find some of his courage, I can't do better.

CHAPTER 12

Second Descent

To Know the Dark

To go in the dark with a light is to know the light.
To know the dark, go dark. Go without sight,
and find that the dark, too, blooms and sings,
and is traveled by dark feet and dark wings.

—Wendell Berry

When Delia gave me her retirement gift, Stephen Levine's *A Year to Live*, I was inspired to explore the possibility of my own death. To my surprise I wasn't afraid of death. Instead I felt loss, a profound grief that, if I were to die soon, I would lose all my wonderful friends and family. I would have to give up everything I love about living. It was as though my cello, my grandchildren, the birds at the feeder, the beach, the woods, and even the sunlight would all be taken from me. One moment I would have them—the next they would be gone. Instead of fear I discovered grief and a profound passion for living.

Then I flashed on another ancient memory . . .

It's my senior year of high school in Saxton's River, Vermont. I'm sitting on damp grass, just inside a quarter-mile cinder track, doing a series of warm-up stretches. To my right are two sets of open bleachers located just outside the hundred-yard straight-away. Fifty feet back from those is a stand of oak and maple rising naked from a heavy bed of last fall's leaves. To my left is the empty football field. Beyond that sit three tired school buildings, their dark imposing weight softened by the green moss growing between the bricks.

The field is scattered with fourteen-to-eighteen-year-olds. A few are jogging around the track, others are doing a variety of pre-race stretches. The sun is filling the western sky with gentle warmth, while a quiet breeze carries the cool moist hint of rotting snow, the last remnants of which are buried in the dense stand of spruce at the far end of the track.

Some of us on the track team have been preparing all year. In the fall, as part of the cross country team, we had run mile after mile along the dirt roads that lace the nearby hills. In the first few weeks I gained speed and stamina, the running becoming fluid and easy. Wherever we went, low granite walls held us in on either side. Each stone, worn round by eons of glacial grinding, had been extracted with horse and sledge to clear the land for farming. Now they lined our route like guardians of our colonial past.

In the pastures beyond the walls were dozens of dun-colored cows, hooves leaving muddy tracks through the grass that converged at the entrance to each farm's milking barn. Between the pastures lay plantations of sugar maple, and, if you looked carefully, you could see the sugar house tucked behind the barn, yet keeping its distance in case of fire. In the early spring, long before the first buds, when the tree sap rose from the roots in full flood, the smell of maple mixed with wood smoke would fill the air, and you could watch thick clouds of steam rise from the roof vents of the sugar house as the farmer wrung the excess water from the gathered sap.

Now that it is late spring, I have switched from cross country to track. In practice I started strong and did well, usually beating my team mates, but today is our first real competition with a neighboring school and I'm nervous and tense. My event, the mile, is the last one of the meet. I've already done my stretches and warm-ups, so I have a long wait. As I sit on the grass, I'm overcome with self-doubt. This is much more serious than the fun of practice. Now it feels as though it's all up to me, that I *must* win the race. What if I don't do well? What if I'm a total flop? What if this is just like the fifth grade science fair where I had failed so miserably? Just the possibility brings a flush of shame to my face. For thirty minutes, these thoughts run screaming through my head. Soon I feel defeated, exhausted before I've begun. As the runners gather for the start, I drag myself to the cinder track, line up with the others and wait for the starting gun. Instead of my usual win I come in sixth, not even placing for the team.

All through the season this pattern repeats itself—winning in practice, losing in competition. The more important the race, the less I'm able to succeed. It's humiliating.

This old memory gave me a firm grasp on a second fear: that, just like the race, if the going gets tough, I will give up—that in the midst of this medical crisis I will arrive at some critical tipping point between life and death and, instead of fighting back, I will give up and die.

Then I remembered an account of young British sailors lost at sea during the Second World War. Those who had a strong will to live had had a far better chance of survival than those who hadn't. Could I find a way to amplify my passion for life, somehow generate a fierce desire to make it through. What would fuel such a drive? What was so powerful and dynamic in my life that, by keeping a clear-eyed view of it, would give me the strength and guts to endure, to swim powerfully upward to the surface where life awaited me? Two answers came immediately: our granddaughter Sierra and my love of hiking in nature.

Being with Sierra is such a delight—abandoning her by dying is unthinkable. Delia and I had been in the hospital the day she was born; we had held her small body in our arms. I had carried her on my shoulders a thousand times. When she was small, I had happily endured endless teasing. While Delia cooked supper and chatted with us, Sierra would climb onto my lap, pull a pen from my pocket and threaten to write all over my face; or she might pull my glasses off and hold them behind her back, grinning the whole time. At other times we found endless pleasure in a small, one-rope swing that dangled from a tree in our yard. I would push, she would tease. Her favorite was to turn just a half turn so her feet were toward me, then she would thrust her socks into my face on the return swing and yell, "Smelly feet!" while I held my nose in mock disgust. We would play this game for hours. Clearly Delia and I were in grandparent heaven.

Now, as the surgery neared, I forged even more powerful links with this child. First I reviewed these memories again and again, cementing them deep inside me, building a reservoir of resource I could easily draw upon in the hospital. Then I made an unspoken commitment not to leave her, a strong clear lifeline to grasp should the moment of drowning ever come.

Likewise, I knew the long slow rehabilitation after surgery could be boring, even depressing—another place where I might get discouraged and quit. So I did the same thing with my love of wilderness and hiking: I took time to remember some of my favorite trips. There was one in particular.

It's a Friday afternoon in September. Julie and I are in our twenties, and we've decided to climb mile-high Katahdin, the tallest mountain in Maine. We leave work early, make the long drive to Baxter State Park, and enter the parking lot just as the last sunlight is kissing the top of a nearby hill. Swinging our fifty-pound packs onto our backs, we start the four-mile ascent to base-camp. With dense forest on both sides and only a sliver of moon, we hike the stony trail by flashlight. Two hours later we arrive at Chimney Pond where we search through the dark for an unused lean-to. There, we throw down our packs, roll out our sleeping bags, and immediately fall asleep.

We awake just as the predawn light begins to sweep the sky with a faint wash of robin's-egg blue. Looking up from the open end of our lean-to we see, rising straight to the zenith from the valley floor, the dark shape of Baxter Peak. In the dim morning light it seems almost close enough to touch. To our left and right, the razor-sharp cliff that forms the rest of Mount Katahdin wraps us in darkness.

"Tom, look," Julie whispers, pointing to our left.

There, not eight feet away, stands a mother moose and her youngster, browsing on a bush. The big one turns her head toward the sound of Julie's voice, sniffs the still air, and slowly ambles off, her offspring at her heals.

By seven we're up and hiking again. To avoid the cliff we take the ridge to our right. There, Cathedral Trail makes a long steep ascent to a saddle just a few hundred yards short of the peak. By the time the sun enters the valley at ten o'clock, we're halfway up. Here we have to scramble almost vertically. Hand over hand we climb, up a huge tumble of room-size boulders. Only the painted trail markers on the rocks keep us from getting lost. It's hard work. Even the small load in our day-packs gets heavy, and we're forced to make frequent stops. Once we make the high saddle, however, the trail became almost flat. It soon leads away from the edge and becomes an easy meander through a grassy plain to the summit.

The top seems disappointing—only an eight-foot cairn at a high point in a rocky field. We wander away. Suddenly, there's the cliff. I look down. Two-thousand feet straight below is the rich blue circle of Chimney Pond and the cluster of lean-tos where we had started that morning. Evergreen forest is everywhere, blanketing the nearby hills and stretching to the horizon.

We sit, entranced. The only sound is the buzz of a few nearby insects. The breeze ruffles my hair. As I run my hands through the bits of grass and moss at my side, the last remains of morning dew wet my finger tips. We lie back, look up, and are drawn into an infinity of blue. Slowly, a thin silver cloud begins to form against the blue, repeating the line of the cliff's edge. The sun, having begun to heat the valley floor, is creating currents of moist air that are sliding up the cliff face and condensing high overhead.

Glancing to my right, I see an eagle fifty feet above the precipice, hovering on that same rising air. "Look," I whisper, "To your right."

Next to me I can hear Julie breathe, "Oooh," as she turns her head to look. Within moments, the bird finds a thermal. Sliding into it, she circles. Higher and higher she rises until she's climbed another thousand feet or so. Without so much as the twitch of a feather, she turns westward and starts a rapid glide. Within moments she's out of sight. As the last speck of her disappears, I realize I have been holding my breath for a long time.

Experiences like this nourish my soul. Anytime I enter the quiet world of true wilderness and nature's wild things I feel replenished. So I made a second vow: All through recovery I would hold trips like these as my goal. That would be my motivation to do whatever it took to regain my strength for a complete comeback.

This felt a lot better, but I was still unsure how I would react if the crunch came.

CHAPTER 13

Vision Quest

Asking Directions in Paris

Où est le Boulevard Saint Michel?
You pronounce the question carefully.
And when the native stops,
shifting her narrow sack of wine and baguettes,
lifting her manicured hand,
you feel a flicker of accomplishment.
But beyond that, all clarity dissolves,
for the woman in the expensive shoes
and suit exactly the soft gray
of clouds above the cathedral does not say
to the right, to the left, straight ahead,
phrases you memorized from tapes
as you drove around your home town
or mumbled into a pocket *Berlitz* on the plane,
but relays something wholly unintelligible,
some version of: *On the corner*
he is a shop of jewels in a fountain
when the hotel arrives on short feet.
You listen hard, nodding,
as though your pleasant disposition,
your willingness to go
wherever she tells you,
will make her next words pop up

from this ocean of sound,
somewhat the way a dog hears its name
and the coveted syllable *walk.*
If you're brave enough, or very nervous,
you may admit you don't understand.
And though evening's coming on and
her family's waiting, her husband lighting
another Gaulois, the children setting the table,
she repeats it all again, another gesture
of her lovely hand, from which you glean
no more than you did the first time.
And as you thank her profusely
and set off full of groundless hope,
you think this must be how it is
with destiny: God explaining
and explaining what you must do,
even willing to hold up dinner for it,
and all you can make out is a few
unconnected phrases, a word or two, a wave
in what you pray is the right direction.

—*Ellen Bass*

W hile reviewing old hikes, I recalled one more experience, a time when I might have quit but didn't.

It's a Saturday afternoon two years before this present crisis. I'm in my office taking a call from Charlie, a tall, powerful Native American who I had met a couple of years before through my friend Tala. She had said, "I think you should come with me to meet my Lakota friend and experience his sweat lodge. He's the real thing."

Charlie is a quiet man with a passion for wilderness and wild things and a deep commitment to use the sweat lodge to help people bring balance to their lives. Many of those who come are recovering alcoholics or addicts, while others are facing inner demons or personal crises. A few come for the companionship of the sweat lodge. Charlie welcomes them all, using the old Lakota chants and ceremony to heal and nurture, replenish and return to harmony.

When I picked up the phone, Charlie said, "Tom, at the end of the summer I'm leading a week-long trek into the Marble Mountains for a sit-fast. Can you come?"

"What's a sit-fast?" I asked.

"That's where you go into a wild place alone to sit and fast for three days and nights."

"Is it anything like a vision quest?" I asked. "That's what I want to do. I've been thinking about one ever since retirement."

"They're different. I don't usually lead vision quests, but you could come and do yours anyway if you want."

"Okay. Where are the Marble Mountains?"

"Just south of the Oregon border and west of Interstate Five. It's a wilderness area with nothing but mountain trails, so we'll be carrying everything on our backs. We might even see bear and mountain lion. You really should come."

I feel far from ready to take on such a challenge, but on impulse I say, "Thanks Charlie, I'll be there."

As I hang up I think, *what am I getting into*? I've never fasted for three days, nor sat alone in the wilderness. I did a few overnights long ago, but never week-long treks carrying everything on my back, and now I'm in my sixties and out of shape.

To get ready, I spend most of the early summer extending my sea-level walks and carrying a weighted pack. In July, Delia and I take a long car-camping trip through the high country of the North West. Besides visiting family in Wyoming and Montana, we spend lots of time hiking. With each trek I load my pack with more weight and walk longer distances up steep trails at altitudes of five to seven thousand feet.

As August approaches I realize there is more to this than a tough body. I want to have some sort of "vision", some clarity that will help guide me through retirement. But my fear is that God or Great Spirit, if they speak to me at all, will speak in such a quiet, small voice that I won't notice, the three days spent alone with nothing happening.

And, of course, Charlie did say "bear and mountain lions". Growing up on an island on the coast of Maine with no deadly predators other than the occasional fox, I could walk anywhere in complete safety, never learning how to deal with either of these big animals. Now the thought of meeting one face to face is damn scary. I've been thinking of getting a big sheath knife for self-defense, but the idea is preposterous. I know nothing of knives as weapons, or of fighting bears. Still, all summer I've been wrestling internally:

I want the knife.

No, that's absurd, and anyway, this is about courage and you should go without one.

I want the knife.

The week just before I leave, I invite some friends to help with the spiritual part of my quest. With Mary Ann's guidance, we prepare prayers for a successful vision quest and for friends, family, or acquaintances who are in need. She shows us how to pray each petition into a pinch of ceremonial tobacco, place the tobacco in the center of a two-inch square of cloth, and wrap the cloth around it to form a tiny bundle. Finally we tie each bundle into a large loop of string so that, when we are done, we have filled the room with a circle of one-hundred and fifty brightly colored prayers. Carrying everyone's appeals in these prayer ties[17] will be an important part of my journey.

Finally August arrives. I drive to Charlie's a day ahead of our early morning departure. The trip is spent obsessing about bears, going over what to do if I meet one on the trail or at the vision quest site. As I drive by a big camping store, my car steers itself into the parking lot and practically pushes me out onto the pavement. Inside, I'm drawn immediately to the knife counter where the best they have is a puny little thing with a five-inch blade. My fears must have wanted some giant fifteen-inch Bowie knife, but I rationalize that I can use this little one as a symbolic blade, one for ceremony that I'll only wear when sitting in prayer in my inner circle. My rationalization is all bull-shit and I'm embarrassed and a bit ashamed, but I buy it anyway.

The next morning there are six of us gathered at Charlie's, packs and gear ready long before sunrise. Two of us will sit on the mountain alone; the other four will be learning from Charlie at base camp and acting as a safety net for emergencies. Shivering in the early morning cold, we climb into two cars and drive the sixty miles to the trailhead, starting down the wilderness path just as the sun comes up.

As we start up the first ridge, we leave the dry summer heat of the valley behind and ascend into cool mountain breezes. The trail is dry and dusty

---

[17]   See Appendix B—Making Prayer Ties

under our feet. Small patches of sunlight filter down through dense green forest. I feel marvelously alive. The trail is quiet and almost empty; we meet only two or three other backpackers. Bear scat is everywhere. Shortly after lunch we start up the second ridge, our fifty-pound packs feeling much heavier. On one of the stops to catch our breath, Charlie draws our attention to a fresh paw print in the dust. It's mountain lion.

By late afternoon the packs are impossibly heavy, but we soon find a place for our base camp in a small open valley with a marshy pond at one end. We are so tired that we prepare only the simplest of suppers. Then, as the others pitch their tents, I spread my sleeping bag in the open a little distance away. It's dusk. Suddenly there are mosquitoes everywhere. Frantically I put on insect repellant, but the bugs are so bad I'm sure I'll be bitten in the night. I quickly crawl into my bag thinking, *I should have brought a tent!* But as I roll over and look up, I see bats zipping about just two or three feet overhead, catching insects against the star-filled sky. In the morning I awake from a sound sleep without a single bite and think, *What a good omen for the challenge ahead.*

Day One of Quest

Early the next morning, with no breakfast, we bushwhack up the mountain side to find my quest site. After a quarter-mile of hopping boulders and wading through brush, we finally find it, a small sun-dappled glade with a huge flat-topped boulder in the center. Colorful wildflowers are scattered through the grass and a cool clear stream runs across the lower corner. Three of the four compass directions are marked by tall, stately trees and the fourth by the gray husk of a once proud pine.

Charlie sings some Native American blessing chants, asking for help and protection during my time alone. We sanctify the glade with additional prayers and a sprinkling of cornmeal around the outer edge, then tie a single colored prayer flag to each of the four trees.[18] Except for a short path to the stream for water, I am not to leave this circle for the next three days and nights. I wave good-bye to my support team and step into sacred space.

---

[18] For most North American Indian Tribes the number four is sacred and figures prominently in their culture, religion, prophecies, and oral traditions or stories. Although there may be some variations from tribe to tribe, the four colors, white, yellow, red and black, represent the four cardinal or sacred directions:

I've brought very little—only the dozens of prayer ties my friends had made, a shamanic rattle, the clothes on my back, water, a sleeping bag and journal, and the knife. While I spread the brightly colored ties in a circle near one edge of my rock I think, *This ancient boulder is so beautiful—it's as though I'm placing all these prayers on God's altar.*

It's afternoon and everything is slowing down. I realize I've been standing in a shady spot in my tiny meadow for a long time without moving. Except for the distant brook, a few insects and an occasional hummingbird, this place is quiet. I take a few slow steps toward my boulder. With each step I lift a foot, help it search for the spot which will create the least disturbance, then slowly let it descend to the firm earth. The sun, which rose ever so slowly to the zenith this morning, is now sinking even more slowly toward the west. Time has become hugely dilated—minutes seem to take hours, until it feels that the day will never come to a close. A small colony of black ants has made its home under a disintegrating log half buried in the soil atop my boulder. I watch them by the hour. I become intimate with the many buzzing insects that fill the air. I'm surprised that none of these ever bother me—they go about their business and I about mine. I'm not shooing them away—they are not biting me.

As I lie awake late into this first night, I am struck by the thought that this stretching and dilation of time is like the dilation of the cervix just before birth. Is stepping into retirement an opportunity for rebirth, a new approach to life?

Day Two of Quest

It's early morning and thirty-two hours into the fast. Even though I constantly think and dream of food, I'm not hungry. Standing up for the first time today, I feel a lot weaker and very dizzy. Using my shamanic training, I sit in my circle of prayer ties and ask Grandfather Mountain for help and for the strength and courage to continue. It has been years

---

North, East, South and West. These colors may also represent the four colors of the human race, and the four elements: Earth, Water, Fire and Air. In addition, green is often used to represent Mother Earth, and blue is used in place of black or to represent water or for the sky overhead.

since I asked for this kind of help, preferring to follow the dictates of the stubborn, independent, Down-East Yankees of my childhood.

Grandfather Mountain directs me to Grandmother Cedar at my west gate. I sit beside her, leaning my back against her rough bark. As I close my eyes and use the rhythm of my rattle to help center me, I begin to imagine her holding me in her protective arms. After a long moment, I hear her say, "Patience my son, it is all about patience and learning to *be* rather than *do*. Sitting in this mountain temple for three days with nothing to do is exactly what you need for your next birthing to occur. In the meantime I hold you as your mother did in her womb."

I've run out of water, so I step over to the brook that runs nearby to get more. (When we created this sacred circle, we had made a gate at the edge of the brook, just so I could do this.) As I bend over to start filtering from the stream, I notice a tiny olive-green frog resting on a stone near my feet. He doesn't move. *Can I get closer?* Ever so slowly I squat next to him. He still doesn't stir. I reach over and lower my finger until it just touches him. I can hardly breathe, don't dare move a muscle for fear he'll leap away. Without willing it, my finger strokes him, then lifts and repeats. His slick moist skin is so thin I can feel each tiny bone of his back. Three times I stroke him. As my finger lifts for the fourth time he leaps into the water and swims downstream out of sight. Awestruck, I gather the water I need and return to the boulder.

By early afternoon the pace of this little circle has slowed so much, it begins to irritate me. *Will this day ever end?* I've taken time to pray, to notice everything in my surroundings, to sit with my four trees—I've even napped three times trying to doze away the hours. No matter what I do the day hangs suspended, time frozen, nightfall a thousand years away. There has always been something to make the hours pass: work at the office, emails to answer, novels to read, house chores to finish—always something . . . . Now there is nothing, an emptiness I cannot fill.

I've made the mistake of bringing my watch. I see that it's 3:36. I sit and track a bee as it makes its way from flower to flower; I look at the trees again; I listen for the sound of the brook. It's 3:39. I enter my inner circle of prayer ties and sit, trying to find that place of inner quiet. It's 3:44. Only five minutes! When is this day going to be over? I'm used to sitting for a long hour in the gathered silence of Quaker Meeting, but thirty hours seem interminable.

It's almost dusk. The stretching of time has become painful, like a hot searing sword cutting through my consciousness, overwhelming everything else. *This is boring, uninteresting, driving me nuts. Sitting here isn't working; I've got to do something!* I leap up, jump down off the boulder, pound my feet in the grass, hardly noticing where I place my boots. I yell, *Damn vision quest, damn Charlie, damn mountain! This is intolerable! I want out, but I've got to stay. If I quit, I'll never live it down. Charlie and my friends at home will think I'm a schmuck.* Meanwhile I'm crashing around, crushing flowers, matting the grass and leaving deep imprints in the soil.

After fifteen minutes of this I cool down, most of the anger having run its course, but there is still some residual tension as I scramble back onto the boulder. *Darn, my ants are leaving.* Abandoning their nest under the rotting log near my bed, a long line of black ants, white eggs held high, are marching single file off the rock as fast as they can go. A moment later a couple of mosquitoes land on my arm and bite, the first bites of the quest. It seems the anger has upset some of the others in this circle. Taking a few deep breaths I attempt to return to a state of inner quiet, that place of sacred space that we created when I first arrived. Soon the insects stop biting. I am at peace again. Meanwhile a soft sadness settles over this little glade, a sorrow for the grass and flowers and tiny soil creatures crushed a few moments ago by my heavy, disrespectful boots.

In the middle of the second night I awake from a dream. In my dream a mountain lion comes bounding out of the woods into the clearing and leaps toward the boulder to attack. One of my power animals appears on the boulder beside me. He confronts the other animal, freezes him in mid-leap, and says, "Stop! You cannot have him. He's mine and I have yet to use him!"

Day Three of Quest

I have made it through the second night, but I'm so weak I can hardly hold up my head to write the dream in my journal. When I stand, I nearly pass out, narrowly missing a fall from the boulder. I sit for a while trying to regain my strength, but instead I start to hallucinate. In my delirium I hear women's voices just out of reach. They seem to be hissing through the insect sounds, washing up from the brook or rustling in the forest leaves beyond my circle. I lean forward, straining to comprehend their message, but it eludes me. Is this the extent of my vision? Am I going to spend three long frustrating days starving myself on this mountain side only to hear some voices I cannot decipher?

Soon I don't feel well. My heart is racing wildly, trying to thump its way out of my chest, yet I haven't moved for an hour. The heartbeat staggers, like the footsteps of some drunken sailor wandering away from the night's bar in search of his sea-legs. *I don't like this. Maybe this much fasting isn't good for this sixty-two-year-old body. Maybe prayer will help.* Carefully, so I won't fall, I move into my circle of prayer ties. There I ask my power animals to lend me their courage, strength, and stamina for this third day and night. Half an hour later, rummaging through my pack for another water bottle, I come across a forgotten chocolate bar. *If I eat it, will I defeat the purpose of my quest, or is this the answer to my morning's prayer?* After a long inner debate I decide in favor of good health and eat it.

By early afternoon I feel better, so I sit for a while with the tree marking my east boundary. He tells me he is the nurturer and the charismatic, teaching younger trees how to grow and live, drawing other trees to him like filings to a magnet. "Use your shamanic training to help others. Become a mentor for those needing guidance. Listen with love to those in grief and pain." Then he reminds me of all my friends at home who have lit candles for my quest. "Be grateful—be thankful. Without their loving support you might have quit yesterday."

I awake in the middle of the third night, look up at the high bright stars surrounding the white river of Milky Way, and realize that the mountain lion dream has come again. Again my power animal repeats his message, "You cannot have him. I have yet to use him!" I lie awake wondering, *How will he use me? Is there some important task ahead?* Finally I drift off to sleep.

Day Four

Early morning of the fourth day, as I roll up my sleeping bag and pack my few things, I realize that I haven't seen any bear or mountain lion. Real ones never appeared at the edge of the woods, nor did I hear them rustling in the more distant brush. Sitting in this circle of spirit, things have felt different; I'm not sure "protected" is the word, but the old dread of bears and mountain lions no longer matters. Certainly my power animal is here to protect me from the inner erosion of my fears, and that seems enough.

After thanking the four trees, my circle, and all of nature's creatures that showed up, I weakly start back to base camp. Half way down I meet Charlie and the others who have been working their way up to find me.

We descend through the trees and undergrowth in near silence. I barely speak. At base camp I'm welcomed with hugs and angelic smiles. For the next few hours the simplest kindness moves me to tears.

For two days we relax at base camp, eating delicious food and enjoying good companionship to restore our energies. The seventh day we make the long hike out to the parking lot and drive to Charlie's, arriving in time for supper. By eight o'clock I am so exhausted I crawl into his guest room bed and immediately fall asleep. At midnight I get up, tiptoe quietly out of the house and start the six-hour drive home.

The road from Charlie's is dark and empty; soon I'm in a deep reverie. It has taken seven days, three alone on the mountain, but I have gotten a small taste of what it is like to slow down enough to actually *BE*. I have *DONE* all my life. I have rushed to my job, worked half-frantically at my desk, kept myself cranked up with cup after cup of coffee, responded to crisis after crisis, then dashed home again. There I would fall asleep exhausted, wake the next morning, climb into my car, and repeat the cycle endlessly.

The mountain has taught me how hard it is to break the addiction to *BUSY*. But by isolating myself far from civilization with nothing but a bag on the ground, the clothes on my back, and a few prayers in my bag, I have succeeded, at least for a few moments, in breaking that addiction. It has been a gift to learn, even if only for a short time, how to do without, how to be in that place of empty acceptance. And how wonderful it has been to be nurtured for a while by Mother Nature, and to be reminded that ultimately it is she from whom we all come and to whom we will all eventually return. Without her, no human would ever exist, and the earth would be nothing but a barren rock, bereft of all the miraculous vitality that three billion years of evolution have provided.

I'm so pleased that I stayed the three days, so happy that I had let my anger burst forth, breaking through the last barriers to deep spiritual silence. On the mountain I had been reminded, again and again, how lucky I am to have such wonderful friends back home. Without them I would not have made it through that difficult second day.

And what of "I have yet to use him?"

My power animal has been my guardian angel, my protector as well as guide. Through these years of shamanic journeying I have slowly learned to trust his guidance and that of all my journey teachers. To contact them is to contact my deepest spiritual self, the wisest place I know. Perhaps these words of his will lead me to some task or tasks of spiritual significance.

Isn't that what life is about in the end, to be used up wisely and well? By the last stroke of midnight, the last breath of this one life—the only one I'll ever have—to know that I have been used well by Great Spirit. Now that would be an accomplishment!

Then I remember the wise old tree of the west, the one with all the young trees gathered close to his roots. He had spoken of being a mentor. What had my friend Joe said on that walk a month ago? We had been reminiscing about our youth. "It's so frustrating now," Joe said. "There's no one left with any real wisdom. When we were younger there were those who set wonderful examples, people who could guide you through life, people who had found some wisdom that rang true. But they're all gone now."

"Perhaps they aren't all gone," I said. "Perhaps, now that we're in our fifties and sixties, it's we who are to become the guiding lights."

Is this what my power animal wants?

* * *

Too soon I become aware that I have reached the outskirts of Redding and the entrance ramp to Interstate Five. Suddenly there are huge double-trailer trucks everywhere. They're blasting along through the dark at horrific speeds, snapping me violently from my reverie. The ones in the left lane are zipping past at seventy and eighty, while those to the right come growling up my tail pipe. Spotlights from hell fill my car with blinding light and push me harder and harder until I too am accelerating violently southward.

The jolt from gentle wilderness, from hours of silence with nothing but the babble of the brook and the hum of insects to this tense high-speed chase, is painful in the extreme. Why are we on this mad dash down the pike? Where are we going? Does any of it matter? What has come to matter has been the quiet commune with nature, the experience of the slow transit of the sun across the sky, quiet conversations with the trees and my newfound reverence for the smallest of the small. In contrast, everything here seems ugly. This horrid scar of Interstate, ripped from the earth to feed our frantic need for speed, has laid waste to a huge swath of Nature's living soil. It feels as if the road, the trucks and the mad pace homeward are tearing up the tender roots I had so carefully begun to sink into that patch of wild mountain earth.

But as I continue south through the dark, I am determined not to be discouraged and to find ways to hold onto the miracle of my wilderness experience. By the time I can see the first faint glimmers of eastern light,

I have come to realize that an important part of the lesson is to find ways to live with the tension between modern culture and wilderness, walking that difficult line with at least some degree of equanimity.

When I get home I continue my weekly walks in nature to keep my soul replenished. Two weeks after the trip, I buy some wildflower seeds. With special prayers for all wild things, Delia helps me plant them in the garden outside my window. Finally I vow to continue in my own small way to fight for wilderness areas, and to defend the many species that inhabit the planet with us but who cannot defend themselves against the onslaught of human progress.

*   *   *

Now that I was facing life-threatening surgery, I thought that the gods, in their mysterious way, had led me to that quest as a way to help. It opened so many possibilities. What if I could create a sacred space that I could take into my hospital room, a space where the fear no longer mattered? What if my power animal's words meant that I would survive because there was important work yet to be done? What if that work was, as the tree in the west had suggested, helping others? And what if that, in turn, was my stonecutter's cathedral? And lastly, what about my exhaustion at the high school track meet, just when I needed to win? If I could stay three days on the mountain despite an overwhelming urge to leave, I knew I would have a much better chance of not quitting if the going got rough in the hospital.

CHAPTER 14

Grendel's Mother

From the Crest (abridged)

... From the crest of the wave
the grave is in sight,
the soul's last deep track
in the known. Past there
it gives up roof and fire,
board, bed, and word.
It returns to the wild,
where nothing is done by hand.

I am trying to teach
my mind to accept the finish
that all good work must have:
of hands touching me,
days and weathers passing
over me, the smooth of love,
the wearing of the earth.
At the final stroke
I will be a finished man.

—*Wendell Berry*

As I continued to explore my fears, I realized that I had always equated death with dying, speaking of them as though they were one entity. I had looked at death; what about dying?

*   *   *

I'm standing in the cool shade of a circle of redwoods that tower high above me. The air is sweet with the moist smell of rich brown soil mixed with needles. Twenty-three of us are holding hands and moving to the rhythm of a chant broadcast from a nearby boom box. A slow dance step carries our circle first to the right, then to the left, then the right again while the choir sings, "Watch and pray with me, watch and pray." For some reason which I cannot fathom I am quietly sobbing. For ten minutes the chant repeats itself over and over, while I try to hide the tears that run down my face and fog my glasses.

I'm half way through a Quaker workshop entitled *Facing Death: Loving Life.* It's a waypoint on my year-long search for how best to spend my retirement. Until now the workshop has been interesting but hardly earth-shattering. This little exercise, however, is different.

At the next break I ask one of the leaders about the chant. She says, "It's called 'Laudate'[19]. It's about the night when Christ is in the Garden of Gethsemane with his disciples, just before he is to be taken before Pontius Pilate and condemned to crucifixion. He is asking them to come and pray with him."

"Well, I've been crying all through it. You've told me what it's about, but I still don't understand why it moves me so much."

"Just sit with it a while. See what happens."

Days later it came to me: when it's my time to die, I want at least one friend with me, someone to just sit in the room and hold my hand. I want them to be present, to pray, and to watch with me for the coming of the Light that will carry me from life into death, from this world into the next.

Now that surgery loomed, I wasn't planning to die, but having friends available seemed important. Perhaps there was a way, either literally or symbolically, to have my friends with me in the hospital. Their gentle presence would calm and reassure me.

The more I looked at this, the more I sensed that having someone with me might be a clue to the last and biggest fear. As I attempted to reach inside, I could feel it lurking just out of reach. What was it? I had some

---

[19]   *Laudate, Music of Taizé*—Veritas Productions, 7/8 Lower Abbey Street, Dublin 1. (Available in many religious stores.)

time reserved to share with my co-counselor Janet. Perhaps with her help I could descend into Beowulf's lake one last time. The next day, as we sat on my couch and she listened to my ramblings, an old, long-forgotten memory came flooding in.

I am small, perhaps seven years old. I'm lying on my back in a white room with three people bending over me. They're strangers. Where are my Mom and Dad? I'm too scared to say anything. One of the strangers places something over my face. I can't see! In the dark I smell a sickening sweet odor. Suddenly I can't breathe! I push up hard, trying to get the thing off my face, but rough hands hold me down. I panic . . . .

I awake in a hospital ward with a terrible sore throat, surrounded by bedridden strangers. I try to cry out but only a weak croak gets past my swollen vocal cords. No one comes.

When I had this tonsillectomy so long ago, my parents had told me nothing—only that I would "have my tonsils out and get to eat lots of ice cream." They didn't explain what that meant or tell me that I would have a very sore throat that bled. They didn't even tell me that, except for one or two brief visits, I would be alone for a week in an unfamiliar place surrounded by strangers.

As this long forgotten memory swept over me, the little boy in me panicked again. Like a drowning man, I grabbed Janet's arm and held on so tightly I nearly tore the sleeve from her blouse. *Don't leave me. Where's my Mom? Why doesn't she come? Why am I here with these old sick strangers?*

Yet even though the little boy was terrified, my adult observer was exultant! At last I had found the big one! I was in a death struggle with the mother of all my fears, forcing it, like Beowulf with the head of Grendel's Mother, to rise to the surface where I could examine it at will and find the antidote.

Now I could see the exact nature of my nightmare. After the operation I'll be returned to my hospital bed completely helpless and extremely vulnerable, while tied to every imaginable tube and I.V. No one will be there to watch over me. There will be some horrible crisis and I will panic, but no one will come.

This was just what I had been looking for. Having named this monster of my fears, I could speak to her, learn what she wanted, calm her and perhaps enter the hospital victorious! But the answer that would reassure this monster lay in another very painful memory from thirty years before.

CHAPTER 15

Watch and Pray

Timothy at Three

L et's return to the interview with Tom Weidlinger that was started in chapter eleven. It's after lunch on a summer's day in 1977. Julie and I have again gathered around TW's tape recorder in her parents' living room on their Montana ranch. He loads a new tape, hands us the mike and turns on the recorder.

Tom Weidlinger (TW):
So what happened that last Tuesday of February, 1975?

Tom (the author):

I was out of town teaching a co-counseling class, so Julie should tell this part of the story.

Julie—holding my hand very tightly:

Okay. Well, Tim had just turned five the month before. We had spent the previous year battling his cancer with four major lung operations and various forms of chemotherapy. Between treatments his life was surprisingly normal. His recovery from each operation had been so fast that he'd even started nursery school in the fall. But recently he'd started sleeping on a mattress in our bedroom because he had been having difficulty breathing, kind of asthmatic.

I had been very tired and so lay down around 5:00 pm and Tim had joined me. I was just falling asleep, when he woke me up by crawling into bed and rasping, "I can't breathe!"

I turned on the light, took one look at him, and thought, "Oh shit!" and ran for some of my old asthma medicine. "Open," I said, and thrust it into his mouth. "Take a deep breath, honey—breathe." Meanwhile I was praying, "Dear God, help him breathe. If he can just get a little of this stuff in. Help him breathe."

Finally the medication relaxed his breathing enough that I could pick him up, dash downstairs to the phone, and call our pediatrician in Peterborough. I described everything, then put Tim on. After only a few seconds the doctor said, "Come in now!"

All the commotion had brought Sue into the room. "Julie, what's happening? What's going on?"

"Tim's in trouble. Tom's away and I've got to drive Tim to Peterborough. Can you stay with our other kids tonight? You can call anyone at the school if you need help."

"Sure. Anything else?"

"Yes. I've got to bundle Tim up because it's snowing out, but call Bonnie. I need her to help with Tim while I drive."

TW:

Who were Sue and Bonnie?

Julie:

Sue was fabulous. She was a high school girl from Sandy Springs, Maryland, whom we had hired the previous summer to help out. She had flown in for a visit during her spring break. Bonnie was a dear friend and the Meeting School's art teacher. She lived barely a hundred yards down the road.

Anyway, in the emergency room the doctor immediately put Tim on oxygen, then gave him some medications to ease his breathing and get him stable. After three or four hours he said, "Because of his history, he needs to be at Mass General. I'm going to put the two of you and a nurse in an ambulance to Boston."

I had a few moments so I called my friend Dottie to see if she would go to the house and wait for Tom.

So Tim and I had this late-evening, eighty-mile-an-hour drive all the way to Boston with the driver using the horns and siren to clear the road of traffic. From where I was sitting, I could see the cars move over to the shoulder in a big wave, then, out the rear, they would swing back onto the road again. Tim, lying on his 'bed', could look out the window and watch. For the first few minutes he was fascinated by the siren and the speed of our passage through the night, but soon he fell sleep and slept the rest of the way.

At Mass General the doctors knew he was coming. One of Dr. Kim's interns met us and x-rayed him, then they took him up to the children's wing and put him to bed. Meanwhile, I went down to the admittance office. What a crazy night! Dozens of people were being admitted. It's a huge hospital, very bureaucratic. After I filled out endless forms, the admitting officer said, "We haven't any beds on the children's wing. We can't admit him before next Tuesday."

I said, "He's already in a bed!" (Laughing)

"But that's impossible," he said. "You can't do that. It's not allowed."

"Well," I said, "Dr. Kim, the surgeon, has admitted him."

"Dr. Kim or any other doctor in this hospital doesn't have the right to do that. You have to go through me."

"Okay," I said, "Call Dr. Kim."

Finally he did. After a brief conversation, he was very nice to me. (Laughter) I don't know what Dr. Kim said, but he can be a very forceful guy, and he really cared a lot about Timothy.

Shortly after I joined Tim in his room, Dr. Kim came to see me. As we stepped out into the hall, he was almost in tears. He said, "Mrs. Snell, I'm so sorry. There's nothing more we can do. We've looked at the x-rays and the tumor has invaded too much of his lung." (Julie is crying a lot through this part of her story.)

I said, "How much time do you think we have?"

"I'm not sure, but probably a few weeks. We can keep Timothy here and make him comfortable, or we can send him back to the Peterborough Hospital where he'll be closer to you."

"What if we took him home?" I said. "I think that's what he'll want."

"We can arrange for an ambulance if you want, or you can drive him home yourselves. Let me know."

"Tom's on his way," I said. "We'll talk to Tim in the morning and see what we want to do."

By this time I wanted to scream. I walked down the hall a ways, then started to pace—up and down, up and down. I felt like a caged animal; I wanted to leave the hospital in the worst possible way. But it was the middle of the night with nowhere to go, and Tim had been so very clear that he wanted me to stay. There was no way I could leave. One of the nurses had set up a cot and blanket in his room, so finally I crawled in with my clothes on and slept fitfully. Tom arrived a couple of hours later.

Tom:

I got home from Brattleboro around 11:30. I was really tired from a late evening class and a long drive. As I walked in I saw Dottie sitting in the living room. "Dottie, what are you doing here? What's going on? Is something wrong?"

"There was an emergency. Julie asked if I would wait for you," Dottie said.

"My God, what happened?"

Taking my hand to comfort me she said, "Tim's having trouble. He and Julie have been rushed to Boston in an ambulance."

"I've got to go down," I said, my voice shaking. "I've got to be there. They're going to need me!"

"Would you like me to go with you? Keep you company?"

"Oh Dottie, that would be wonderful," I said. "Would you? I'm so tired. You could help me stay awake. What about the kids?"

"Sue's here. She'll take care of them."

When we arrived at 2:00 a.m., I was a wired zombie, but I wanted desperately to get to Timmy. I knew the fastest route through the hospital so, with Dottie right behind me, I hurried through the corridors, up the elevator, and straight to the children's wing. "Where's Timmy?" I asked the duty nurse.

"Hello, Mr. Snell. He's in room 510."

Quietly we tiptoed in and woke Julie. When we stepped out into the corridor, Dottie gave Julie a big hug and I took her hand. "What's happened?" I said. "What did the doctors say?"

"Tom, thank God you've come. I've been frantic. This is it—there's nothing more they can do. We can keep him here or take him home."

Soon we were both sobbing. Dottie had her arms around us. My whole body buzzed with tension and fatigue. My mind was so numb I couldn't absorb what Julie was saying. Finally we went back into Tim's room and tried to rest for the coming day.

TW:

What did you decide to do?

Julie:

As a last-ditch effort the doctors had been giving Tim a horrible drug that forced him to drink fluids almost constantly. It was horrible. (Crying) Now that had stopped, so I said, "Tim, there's nothing more the doctors can do, so from now on you're the boss. Nobody's going to make you eat, or drink, or take any medication. Nobody's going to do any medical procedure unless you want them to."

He gave me a big grin. He knew exactly what it meant to be boss, and that delighted him.

Tom:

"Tim," I said. "Here's your first choice. You can stay here or you can go back to the Peterborough Hospital or we can take you home. What would you like?"

"I want to go home."

So I went and got the car while Dottie and Julie bundled him up against the February cold. We were so nervous about his condition, we weren't even sure we would make it home, but luckily nothing happened.

We got home around ten that morning and put him in the big queen-size bed in our room. Sue sat with him while we got everything organized. Tim had lost a lot of weight, so he looked very thin. We put a pretty flowered sheet on the bed, propped him up with about six pillows and then wrapped him in his blue cotton quilt. He refused to wear any clothes except the red baseball cap that covered his baldness. He was more comfortable that way and it kept people from fussing with him. After a couple of days, even the baseball cap came off.

We got his toys from his room and set him up with oxygen and quite a few steamers. The steamers made the room very humid and they hissed constantly, but they helped with his breathing. He liked what he called "the monk records[20]", quiet male voices accompanied by guitar, so we added our record player from downstairs. Every few minutes he would pick up one of his Matchbox cars and run it back and forth over the quilt. Then he would stop and lie back against his pillows, exhausted from the effort.

At first we slept on a mattress near his bed, but as we got other people sitting with him through the night, Julie and I moved into one of the small rooms at the back of the house.

TW:

What did you tell your other children?

Tom:

No one had told the other three kids what was happening—they just bundled them up and got them on the bus for grade school. So we left Sue and Bonnie with Tim and went early to pick them up. We told them on the way home. Tamara kept asking, "When are you going to tell Tim? You told us. Don't you have to tell Tim?"

And Sarah said in that little-kid's teasing, sing-song voice, "I'm going to te-ll Tiii-mmy. I'm going to te-ll Tiii-mmy."

I thought, *oh God, one of them is going to tell him. Sarah will say, "Hey Tim, you're dying."*

Julie:

Yeah, it got pretty dicey. Finally we explained to them that Tim didn't want to talk about it. We knew not to flood Tim with information, just to answer any questions he had as honestly and directly as we could. If he didn't bring it up, we didn't talk about it.

Tom:

We told them that they could go to school or stay home. They could stay at Bonnie and Wade's next door, or they could go to Maine with the Maine grandparents. They all wanted to go to school and tell everybody. Julie called the teachers to tell them what was going on. Our kids were very open, so the other kids got a day-by-day, blow-by-blow report of what was happening.

---

[20] *Winter's Coming Home, Songs to Celebrate Winter and Christmas by the Monks of Weston Priory.* Recorded at a Benedictine monastery in Weston, Vermont—www.westonpriory.org

TW:

How old were they at this point and how did they relate to all this?

Tom:

By this time Chris was ten and Sarah was six. Tamara and Tim had both had birthdays in January—she was now nine and he was five.

Julie:

Chris spent quite a lot of time with Timothy. He would come home with all these treasures from his fifth grade friends. He would empty out his pockets with all the grubby little worn-out things that ten-year-old boys carry around in their pockets. He would sit down with Timothy and say, "Michael Lambert gave you this; Tom Coburn sent you this." Tim didn't know any of these kids except he had heard his big brother talk about them, but it was very important to him. We got him a tray where he kept them all. He didn't have the energy to play with them, but about two or three times a day he would take inventory. He knew if a single eraser was missing, even though he had about ten of them. He would touch each object and say who had given it to him.

Sarah and Tamara were different. Sarah was only in first grade. The whole thing was much less real to her, and she spent very little time in Tim's room. She was at school during the day and was part of the household downstairs when she was home. Tamara, the one in the middle, kind of freaked. She would look in once in a while but wouldn't sit with Timothy. Tamara loved to draw. She and Bonnie, the Meeting School's art teacher, had become good friends, so Tamara preferred to spend her after-school time at Bonnie and Wade's next door.

TW:

How did the two of you cope? Did you have any other help?

Tom:

Well, as you know, TW, there are sixty of us at the Meeting School, all living in half a dozen farm houses scattered along a three-hundred yard stretch of dirt road. We all pitch in. Students alternate chores with studies—text book in one hand, cook book in the other. I teach in the basement of another house, while Julie teaches in our living room. During classes she sometimes holds our latest infant to her breast while the students discuss the Tudor Kings or *Catcher in the Rye*. We are a tight-knit Quaker community and nearly everyone has found a way to help.

Julie:

Yes, everyone was amazing. Even Marta, a student who had graduated, flew in from Michigan. She had lived in our house for two years. She was close to me and loved our kids. Mother and Daddy and my sister, Helen, flew in from Montana. I was particularly glad that Helen had come. She and I are really close. Her presence was so reassuring!

Tom:

Yeah, it was such a good group. In a couple of days, we had a rotation schedule with pairs of people on eight-hour shifts. Their only job was to be with Tim and to support each other. These pairs were never alone—there was a whole crew—cooking, running errands, and helping out in a million ways.

We didn't have a lot of beds, so most of us hot-bunked: When people needed to sleep, they slept in any bunk that was empty. When somebody went off-duty, they woke the next crew and crawled into their warm bed. People were sleeping in rotation all over the house.

Some came and stayed a while, filling in where they could. Others came but got freaked out and left. But nearly all would contribute something. It was a real community effort.

TW:

How were people freaked out?

Julie:

Well, Tom's parents were an example. They came the first weekend and stayed about two days. When his mother tried sitting with Timothy, she kept patting him and saying "Poor dear, poor dear." He couldn't take it and told her to get out of the room. When he went into one of those breathing things, she would say, "Don't you think you ought to call the doctor and get Tim to the hospital?" She couldn't let go of him. She couldn't say that it's okay for him to die right here and right now. Of course we all had things like that, but it was so strong in her that she couldn't control it.

Tom's father wandered around, not knowing how to fit in or make a contribution. He would sit in the living room really quiet and drawn into himself.

Tom:

Yeah, they were taking so much time and energy that I finally said, "Why don't you go home. There's no reason why we all have to be here getting worn out. We'll need you later when this is all over. We'll come to Maine in a while, and you can take care of us and give us a bit of vacation."

TW:

Did you ever get into arguments? How did you resolve difficulties?

Julie:

Sure. I remember one time . . . Each morning, when our children were getting ready for school, they would squabble and tease and carry on. This particular morning, though, it got really bad. They weren't getting anything done and were going to miss the bus. It was hell. At different times that morning, Mother and Tom and I each bawled the kids out. We each told them very different things, leaving them totally confused.

When we realized what had happened, we got really mad at each other. Mother said it was just ridiculous to have children in the house. We ought to ship them off to their other grandparents. Then Tom got upset.

Tom:

Yeah, I was almost yelling. I didn't like the way Julie's Mom was talking to our kids and I told her so. Then, really exasperated, Helen said, "Well, I'm only trying to do what I can." I can't remember what Julie said. It got very heated.

Julie:

Thank God it didn't last, because suddenly, out of the blue, we looked at each other and started to laugh. That broke the tension. So that's when we put our heads together and came up with some pretty good answers.[21]

First, Tamara was getting more and more temperamental, so we decided she would move in at Bonnie and Wade's. She could visit whenever she wanted, but she would eat and sleep there.

Then Mother offered to get the kids off in the morning. That would be her only responsibility and the kids got only one boss.

---

[21] Decisions at The Meeting School are arrived through Quaker dialog and what's called The Meeting for Business and Worship, processes that can help a group come to agreement on difficult issues. Although we weren't using those techniques directly, I think having experienced them helped us work together smoothly.

Then we said, we've got to take care of ourselves. So we decided that every morning Tom would go to each of us and say, "What are you doing to take care of yourself?" If someone was in bad shape, Daddy would offer to take them out to a lavish lunch or dinner. We tried to figure out who was tired and who needed extra sleep. If there weren't enough people in the house, someone would call out for help. It worked really well and settled things down a lot.

TW:

Was Tim peaceful? Did he have any more breathing difficulties?

Tom:

Usually he was peaceful. He had so little energy he did very little. Every so often, though, he would have one of those respiratory things where his breathing would become labored and scary. Between labored breaths he would wheeze, "I want everybody to come pray!"

One of the people sitting with him would step into the hall, lean over the railing, and call across the open living room to whoever was downstairs. "Tim's having another bad time. He wants everybody to come."

Everyone would gather in a circle around him. We would hold hands and bow our heads in silent prayer. When the house was full, there might be ten or twelve of us there.

Julie:

Sometimes it took quite a while before he was okay. Someone would help him with the oxygen, regulating the flow and holding the mask, while the rest of us prayed. Meanwhile he would fight with the most incredible vigor. You could see him amassing his energies to fight his way through.

TW:

Was he convulsive?

Tom:

No, just pulling for breath, like an asthmatic.

Finally he would get through it. He would look up and give us this . . . . (Sobbing) After all this struggle, he would give us this incredibly serene, quiet smile and say, "I'm okay. You can leave now." (More crying) Then he would lie back and go to sleep.

TW:

Did you ever talk about dying with Timothy?

Julie:

During those last two weeks, it didn't come up directly but I gave him every opportunity. The closest he came (sobbing) . . . one day he said, "This lump is doing something terrible to me, isn't it, Mommy?"

I said, "Yes, it is." (Sobbing) He looked at me and turned away. He didn't ask for any explanation.

Weeks before, we had an incredible conversation, probably in November. He was feeling pretty good and we were between operations. I was settling him down for a nap and he said, "Am I going to die?"

"Well, I don't think so, but it's a possibility. As long as we're fighting this cancer thing, it's a possibility. We don't know whether we're going to win or not."

Then he wanted to know, "What is dying like?"

"Well," I said, "it's like leaving the house and not living there anymore. You're going to leave your body and not live in it anymore. Your body won't have any more feeling."

He thought about that for a while. Then he said, "Well, where do I go? If I don't live in my body anymore, where do I go?"

I said, "Well, God will come and take you to a place that is very nice. You'll be with people that you know but who have died, like David Foster and Phyllis Kerry, Aunt Sarah and Uncle Grant. They will be there to meet you, to make you feel loved and comfortable."

He said, "Will you be there?"

"I'll come later—when I die, but no, I won't be there, because I have to stay here as long as I'm in this body."

When I said that, he crawled into my lap and started to cry. He didn't like the idea of being separated from me. While I held him I said, "You'll be a spirit, a soul, and you'll be able to come back and feel me, but I won't necessarily know that you're there. You can come back and be with me anytime you want. I'll kind of know you're there, because I believe in life after death, and I know that you can do that, even though I may not be aware of you the way I am aware of you sitting in bed with me right now."

"What about Daddy?"

"Well," I said, "he doesn't believe in life after death, so he won't know that you are there the way I do. You can still come and be with him; and when he dies, he will come and find you. There'll be a time when we'll all be together again."

He thought about that for a long time, and then he came up with the most incredible thing for a four-year-old. He said, "Well, that's like God, isn't it? God is spirit and God feels you all the time, but you don't feel him except once in a while."

And I thought, "Wow. Yeah. That's what it's like." He was upset at the idea of separation, and of leaving what was familiar and going someplace else, but he really understood.

TW:

What sort of things was Tim doing?

Tom:

By this time Tim didn't have very much energy. He would listen to the monk records or draw a little, or visit briefly with the kids when they came home, but mostly he slept.

Sometimes, when we were gathered for dinner, he would want to join us. I would wrap him up, hold him close with his head on my shoulder, and carry him down to the big beanbag cushion near the dining room table. In about five minutes he would have had enough, and I would carry him back up. Memories of holding him close like that are so poignant now.

Once in a while he would have a very grandiose idea about what he wanted. Perhaps it was the second week? He said, "Daddy, I want a popgun. Take me to Jaffrey so we can get a popgun."

I thought, *oh my God, we'll never make it. The stress of the trip will be too much.* Then I thought, *But he really wants to do this. I'll be damned if I'm going to say, "No". So he dies on the way in. He's going to die anyway. Who am I to deny him this trip for a popgun?* I was scared shitless, but I said, "Well Timmy, we'll see what we can do."

So I talked to the others. I knew I couldn't do it alone. If I was driving, someone would have to be with Tim, especially if he had a breathing attack. But no one would go with me. It was too much. So I drove to town and brought back a cap-gun. It broke my heart not to take him with me, nor to find exactly what he wanted, and I still regret not finding a way.

TW:

Did you have any outside visitors, people who weren't part of your support team? How were they affected?

Julie:

Near the end of the second week, my friends the Dodds drove up from Boston. The husband had been my family's minister in Red Lodge, Montana and had presided at my sister Helen's wedding and baptized Christopher. After lunch we all went upstairs to visit Tim. After a few minutes Tim started having respiratory difficulty and asked everyone to pray. People trouped upstairs and the Dodds joined us, circling Tim in bowed silence. At one point Tom was looking at Timothy instead of having his head bowed and Tim said, "Daddy, you too. Everybody pray!" About ten minutes later he said, "When is it going to be over? Tell God to make it better." Everyone was crying. Everybody always cried when he did that, because you never knew whether it was the end or not. Finally he got through it all right, gave us his big smile, and fell asleep.

It blew the Dodds away. They left about 3:00 p.m. On the way out Reverend Dodd said, "I have been a minister for a long time and I have counseled a lot of people. I have done pastoral care with families in trouble and families dealing with death. But I have never seen anything like this! The spirit and feeling in this house, the way people work with each other and love each other and hold each other, and the way you all gather around and pray . . . And Timothy's incredible. To see a five-year-old kid who is dying in that state of mind. It's as though he's a little one-hundred-year-old prophet, sitting in that bed with the serenity of a Tibetan Lama. I'll never forget this."

TW:

How about people in town?

Julie:

Well, one afternoon I got a phone call from a woman in Jaffrey, about five miles away. She's a born-again Christian. She has two sons who have played a lot with both Chris and Tim. She said, "Can I come and pray with Timothy? I don't want to come, but God has told me I must."

I asked Timothy and he said, "Okay," so she came that evening. When we went upstairs, Tim was propped up as usual against his pillows and drawing quietly on a piece of paper I'd given him.

About four of us gathered around and held hands in our usual Quaker silence[22]. Meanwhile, the neighbor put a hand on Tim's head and prayed, sometimes in English, sometimes in tongues. It wasn't passionate or hysterical or enthusiastic, just quiet. Tongues has a lovely singsong sound,

---

[22]   See Appendix D—Religious Society of Friends (Quakers)

very quiet and beautiful. In English, she said something like, "Jesus, take this child. Make him whole and bring him health. We ask you to bless him." Then she said, "Jesus, take care of his parents, Tom and Julie. Bless his older brother, whom you have cured of cancer, that he may not be hurt and scared by this experience. Bless his two sisters, Tamara and Sarah, and make them whole." All through this Tim kept scribbling on his piece of paper. Finally she finished.

As she was leaving, she pulled me aside and told me how she had been so scared about coming to this house where it seemed this little child was dying and must be in agony. She had felt critical and angry with us, thinking we had done the wrong thing and that he should be in the hospital. It had gotten so bad she didn't think she could come.

"But God just wouldn't leave me alone," she said. "He told me I must go to your house and pray for Timothy. So I went. The minute I walked in the door I realized how utterly wrong I had been. As I stepped inside I felt an incredible peace. All of you were doing normal things. Your children were happy and smiling and glad to see me. Your mother greeted me and smiled; your sister was so peaceful. Then, when I saw Tim in bed, I knew that I didn't have to feel sorry for him ever again. I know why God wanted me to come here: not because Tim needed me, but because I needed to be healed of my judgment of you and my fear of dying."

TW:

What were some of your greatest fears?

Julie:

I was absolutely terrified of being with Tim the moment he died. There was one day when I couldn't go into his room I was so scared! I was fighting the fear all the time.

TW:

Did you express this to other people?

Julie:

Oh yes. My regular co-counselor came every day and I sure told him! The first day when he came I jumped into his lap, made him hold me, and shook for an hour.

One day in the second week, Tim had a particularly bad time. Afterward I found that I was avoiding his room. My sister, Helen, was in the same state. She looked at me at supper time and said, "You know, I'm not going back into that room!"

So I said, "What are we going to do about it?"

"Your counselor is coming tonight," she said. "Why don't we try a session and see what happens."

When he arrived, we took him into one of the rooms at the far end of the house, closed the door, and did a three-way that was incredible. We got into real screaming and shaking. We would yell about all the awful things our imaginations could conjure up and then we would laugh hysterically and cry and laugh again until it broke its hold on us. Our poor co-counselor had his hands full.

Afterwards I was able to go back; in fact I didn't want to leave. I knew that I had to relinquish him—that I had to let him go—but that was *so* hard. That's part of helping a person die—letting them know that the people they leave behind are okay.

TW:

Were there other fears?

Julie:

I was really afraid I wouldn't be able to stick it out, that in Tim's hour of greatest need I would abandon him. The day that I couldn't force myself to go into his room was a turning point. Beyond that day, I never physically ran away, and I don't think I did emotionally either. But I was fighting it the whole time. I was afraid I wouldn't be able to witness his agony anymore. Part of me wanted to hold my breath, close my eyes, and wake up with it all over. Helen told me of one bad time when she held my hand, looked the other way, and sent her thoughts out into space. Wasn't in that room at all.

Tom:

I don't remember having those feelings, probably because I didn't sit with him so much and didn't let my imagination jump ahead to what might happen. I felt a lot of confidence in Julie and the others who were sitting with Tim and I kept myself busy doing chores, running errands and managing the household.

TW:

Weren't you ever angry?

Julie:

Yes. For the first six months of his illness.

TW:

What were you angry at? How did that come out?

Julie:

I was furious at God! If I could have kicked him I would have! (Laughter) I mean, how can you give me two sons with cancer? That's just not fair! What are you trying to pull?

TW:

Did you have any discussions like that with anyone?

Julie:

Yeah, with God all the time. I would cry and ball him out, and cuss him! I was so mad! Outraged! Outraged that I would have to go through this again. "You dumb God. I passed my test already with Christopher's cancer! You screwball, get off my back! Tim is such a beautiful child and he is going to be such a fantastic adult. What are you doing to us?"

TW:

Weren't you short with the kids or with Tom?

Julie:

I don't think I was very much. This was the value of co-counseling. Tom and I each had co-counselors that we shared time with. Nearly every day we were able to yell and scream and rage, and do it effectively enough that we didn't have to bring it home to the rest of the family.

Tom:

Yeah. These folk were unbelievably generous of their time.

But to answer your earlier question, TW, I don't remember being that angry. What I remember most was feeling scared and anxious—anxious about whether we were making the right decisions and afraid of the implications of Tim's illness. For example, the last kind of chemotherapy they used was horrible stuff. It put terrible demands on all of us. Every day I agonized over it: should we stay with the chemo or should we stop? Here we are two years later and it still gnaws at me.

TW:

Julie, tell me more about your relationship with God[23].

Julie:

For me, and this is probably different than for Tom, a large part of the personal experience was this thing with God. I'm put together in such a way that God is real for me. I talk to him and he talks to me, and I hear

---

[23]   For Tom's approach at the time, see Appendix D.

what he says in all kinds of ways. Not only directly by receiving guidance or through prayers, but also in the things that happen in my life. I see all this as communication between us. What I do is an expression of what I am thinking or feeling toward God. What happens to me is his telling me how he wants me to grow, or what direction he wants my life to take.

My prayers and spiritual guidance never told me the outcome—would Tim live or die? But they did give me reassurance that everything that was happening was ultimately okay. Tim's body was being destroyed, but as a person he was so whole . . . When I saw him taking these experiences in his stride the way he did, I couldn't do anything but marvel.

My sister Helen's the same way. Even though she's two years younger, we're like twins in lots of ways. This relationship with God and spirit is one of them.

TW:

Tell me about that Tuesday, the eleventh, two weeks after you brought him home.

Julie:

It started out like all the other days. Dottie and I went on duty at about seven a.m. When I went upstairs, Tim's room was an absolute mess. Everybody who had stayed with him overnight had left their books, their shoes and belongings, and their plates of half-eaten food all scattered around. The place was stinky and smelly, and Tim looked grungy.

Dottie and I did a real cleanup. It was probably the first real cleanup in the two weeks since we brought Tim home from Mass General. We took everything out: all the dirty dishes, everyone's stuff and all the extraneous things that Tim wasn't interested in any more. We vacuumed the floor, put clean sheets on the bed, and cleaned the pillowcases. The room looked really nice when we got through. I wanted to give Tim a bath, but he wouldn't let me.

Dottie and I sat on his bed for a while and talked. Then Tim said, "No talking in my room, I'm going to sleep. Be quiet, Mommy," so we sat quietly for a while and kept him company. One of the monk records was playing softly in the background and soon Tim drifted off.

My dear friend Jane had come up from Boston. Jane's goal for the day had been to get me out of the house. I hadn't left the house in ten days and everyone was saying I should go. The doctor had come the night before and said that Tim was still very strong, so we thought it would be at least a couple more weeks, maybe even a month or two. I needed to get out, but I didn't want to leave. For two hours I kept saying to Jane, "I'll come with you in just a minute."

Finally, Jane said, "I can't wait any longer. I've got to get home." Tom had driven the twelve miles into Peterborough to get a new oxygen tank, but there were others in the house so, with Tim sleeping peacefully, I said, "Okay, I'm coming."

CHAPTER 16

Winter's Coming Home

T om Weidlinger's tape had run out, so after a ten minute break we all gathered again in the living room.

TW:

Let's continue where we left off. It's mid-afternoon of March 11, 1975 and both of you have left the house.

Tom:

I remember that day so vividly. I remember struggling to get the big oxygen tank out of our old Dodge van. I remember how my wool mittens kept slipping on the smooth steel, and the heaviness of the tank. There was ice underfoot from a recent rain and I had to be careful. Finally I got it inside the pharmacy. When I asked for a new tank, the woman behind the counter paused, whispered something to the druggist's assistant, then said, "You will have to wait—they're not ready."

Julie:

Jane and I drank tea at the Corner Kitchen. I made myself talk to Jane about the Meeting School and our jobs and only a little about Timothy. We stayed for forty-five minutes. The whole time I kept thinking, *Let's get the hell out of here. Tim needs me!* Finally we paid the bill and started home.

Tom:

They made me wait forever. I remember one of the drugstore staff staring at me, then looking away. Outside, I could see half-melted snow banks lining the sidewalks. A few trees were pushing barren branches toward a gray sky.

Julie:

When Jane drove us back to Bonnie's where Jane was staying, I stepped inside for a moment to say hi to Tamara. She seemed very happy and relaxed, so I started to walk home. Just as I went out the door, I said to Bonnie's friend, Wade, "How's Timothy doing? Have you heard anything?"

He looked at me calmly and said, "I think he's left."

"What do you mean, he's left?"

He said, "I don't know. Chris called on the phone and I asked him how Tim was. He said, 'Tim's left,' but I don't know what he meant by that."

Tom:

After a while I saw the pharmacist come in. He hung up his heavy coat, then took me aside and said, "I'm sorry you've had to wait so long. It took me a while to get here, and I wanted to be the one to talk to you. Your wife's sister called. They have been trying to reach you."

"Why would they call?" I said. "I'm going home as soon as I get a new tank."

"You won't need the tank. They want you to come home because Timothy died twenty minutes ago."

Julie:

My mind balked. I couldn't understand what happened. Everything had been fine. So I started home on the icy road. In my mind's eye I was running and slipping, then trying to crawl home. But, I could only see myself slide about, getting nowhere. So I walked very carefully, inching my way forward step by step over the ice. Everything was so stark and vivid: the silhouette of the black branches against the trees, the trees against the gray sky, and the sighing of the wind in the branches.

Tom:

I felt a huge hand reach inside my body and squeeze. Everything clamped down so hard I could hardly breathe. I turned and staggered out the door and into the van. I turned the heater way up, but couldn't get warm.

I was so incredibly angry! I grabbed the steering wheel and shook it. I wanted to shove the gas peddle down through the floor, to peel out of the parking lot and lay a mile long strip of rubber behind me. But I did just the opposite. I drove cautiously on the slick road and watched the trees slide slowly by. I thought, *the trees look so sad in their grey nakedness. Look at the little birches. They're all bent over, bowed to the ground in their grief.*

Julie:

Going up our driveway, I rehearsed everything: How I was going to take off my coat and boots and mittens, how I was going to get up to his room . . . . I had every motion figured out. *What if my jacket zipper gets stuck? I'll have to walk to the kitchen, get the scissors out of the drawer, and calmly cut the whole jacket off!* I was so calculated and controlled—no panic at all!

Tom:

In the driveway there was ice everywhere. As I walked toward the door, I wanted to scream. I wanted to yell, *Tim, I'm coming; I'm almost there. Wait for me—I'll be there soon . . .*

Julie:

The house was quiet. The oxygen and steam, all those things that had gone SSSHHHHHH for two weeks, were turned off. Mother, Helen, Sue, Martha, Bonnie and Chris were all in the living room. Helen met me at the door. She looked very happy. As she hugged me she said, "Tim left when you were gone. It was very beautiful. You want to go upstairs and see him?"

Then Mother came and held me too. Nobody cried—everybody looked peaceful—like they'd been zapped. I did my little act of taking off my boots and jacket, then went upstairs. He looked just the way I had left him except even more lovely, as though he was carved out of sleeping marble.

I opened the window because it was still steamy and close. One of the monk records was playing *Winter's Coming Home*. I sat in the room alone with him for a while, touching him and kissing him and crying.

Tom:

When I went in, the house seemed so quiet. There were people downstairs but I didn't stop. I went straight up. For a moment I couldn't go in. When I did, I sat on his bed and cried, my tears soaking the quilt that covered him. *Timmy, all your hair's growing back. It's so soft and new, and you're so warm, and I'm so sorry I've failed you, that I couldn't make it better.*

Then I noticed the open window and beyond it a sunset that was pulling its colorful blanket over the entire western sky. I thought, *He's gone to join the sunset.* And I wept some more.

TW, after a pause:

Let's take a break and come back in ten minutes.

*   *   *

TW:

Okay, now that we're back, tell me about the rest of that day.

Julie:

I can't remember Tom coming very well, but I remember that at some point we went upstairs and held each other at the foot of the bed. Then Tom sat with Tim for a quite a while. All afternoon I would sit with Tim for a few minutes, then leave. I would go downstairs, then be immediately drawn back up again. I was constantly moving back and forth.

Tom:

Yeah, it was the same for me—upstairs to sit or touch him and cry, then downstairs to make phone calls or fill out undertaker forms, then upstairs again.

Julie:

After things settled a little I helped Chris while he held Tim's hand and said things like, "Tim, are you there? Are you gone Tim?" Then Tamara came up. She said, "Mommy, why did you open the window? Did you open it to let his soul out?" Then she looked at Tim and said, "Mommy, he looks awful. Is he going to stink tomorrow?"

Our local doctor came around supper time to fill out the death certificate. When he went upstairs, I put my arm around him while he stood at the end of the bed and cried.

Tom:

In the evening, after the funeral director came to take Tim's body, Bonnie and Helen shared with us what had happened. The two high school girls, Sue and Marta, members of our basic crew for the past two weeks, had been sitting with him. Christopher and Tamara had looked in after school, then left. Moments later Timothy pushed his oxygen mask away. Sue tried to put it back, but he pushed it away again, rather forcefully this time. Even though Tim seemed okay, Sue realized things weren't normal and nearly panicked. Marta ran to get Bonnie and Helen who took over, while Marta and Sue moved to the foot of the bed. As Helen took his hand, he looked up at her with an incredible look that seemed to say, "It's okay." As they continued to hold his hands, they said things like, "It's okay Tim, you can leave now. We're here with you, it's okay to go."

There seemed to be an inward concentration about him, almost as though he were willing himself to go. While they talked, he closed his eyes. In a little while the color left his skin—as though he left his skin first. Soon he stopped breathing. There was no struggle, no anxiety, no trauma; there was no gagging or any of the nonsense that the doctors had talked about. After a few more minutes his heart stopped. All through it they held his hands and kept saying, "You're doing fine, Tim; you're doing beautifully."

After a while there was a feeling that he needed space, so they let go of his hands but continued sitting on the edge of the bed. At some point someone started the monk record again. Finally, they turned off all the steamers and went out and closed the door.

Julie:

Helen said that nobody cried until I came home. Instead there was a sense of incredible peace. It was as though Tim had filled the whole house, that he had left his body but didn't leave the house for a long time. Helen's guidance told her that it was a very special crossing, and that there were an incredible number of souls on the other side waiting to receive him.

Later, in the evening, after Tim's body had been taken away and everyone had settled down, I lay down on the big beanbag cushion in the living room and started to cry. Dottie came and held me and stroked my hair. I must have spent half an hour in her arms crying my heart out.

Tom:

At bedtime, Julie and I were both wound up and exhausted. We thought of going upstairs, but there was no way that we were going back to our bedroom where Tim had been for the past two weeks. So Julie and I went to sleep on the living room carpet with our heads on the big beanbag pillow. Julie's mother and Helen went upstairs. I'm not sure where the others were.

I don't know if there was a thunderstorm, or what, but at some point in the night, we woke up to find that everyone, except Julie's parents, was lying with their heads on the big pillow. They had come with their blankets and clustered around us in the dark, as close as they could without disturbing us.

*   *   *

The first evening after Tim came home from the hospital that last time, an owl appeared in the tree just outside our front door. Every evening, whenever someone arrived, they would listen for it, and every night someone would hear its mournful cry. Soon it became the topic of evening conversation—who had heard the owl? Had it missed a night? No. Had anyone heard it before Tim came home? No. What did it mean? Then, the night Tim died, the owl left. Even though we listened carefully, it didn't return.

Two weeks later, as I washed for breakfast, I felt anxious for Tim, hoping that his passage had been an easy one. I thought, *I wonder how he's doing*? A moment later I heard the owl for the first time since that fateful afternoon. *How wonderful. The owl's telling me he's all right!*

Only years later did I realized that this was my first introduction to the world of mystery and the shamanic experience. All I knew then was that my anxiety for Timothy had been eased.

*   *   *

A few months ago I got two e-mails from Sue. After Tim's memorial service, she had returned home to her parents and to high school. We had corresponded once or twice—then I didn't hear from her for years until the e-mails came. This is the second message.

Dear Tom,

> If you got my last e-mail, you know that I've been a hospice nurse for many years. I don't remember if I wrote before or after I took over the pediatric dept. of our hospice, but anyhow, here I am, hospice coordinator and case-managing three kids.
>
> The child who is sickest right now, a 16-year-old girl, lives in my neighborhood, and I see her one or two times a day. As I left her house yesterday, and drove to [Quaker] Meeting, I thought a lot about Timothy and the incredible care he received from your family and community. I realized that when I am at my very best as a hospice nurse, it comes directly from the gifts that I received from all of you during that time.
>
> I spent four years in nursing school and learned a lot about anatomy and pathophysiology; then I learned how to apply the book learning in my first years of adult hospice. A couple of years ago I felt drawn to pediatrics and went to work for the Navy (the last place you'd expect to find a lesbian Quaker), where I was trained and certified in pediatric chemotherapy. Now I find myself where I believe I was destined to be since the day I met Timmy.
>
> I write to you now from the kitchen table of Linda's house. Her family is having private time with her. By the time you read it, I believe that she will be gone. She's not in pain or any

other physical distress thanks to my training in pharmacology, but the best part of her care comes from being at home with her family. I am in awe of the strength that her parents have, after a very long fight to save her, and at the love that their community surrounds them with.

The days here are very much like yours were with Timmy. Two people sit with Linda at night, one awake, one dozing but available, in four-hour shifts. Lots of junk food around. Lots of people. Controlled chaos. The only difference is the presence of the hospice team: me fine-tuning the meds, assuring the family that Linda is comfortable, explaining the meaning of physical changes, teaching them ways to care for her; Barbara, the social worker, working with the other kids, teaching the family ways to support each other; Phyllis, the pastoral counselor; and Margaret, the volunteer, offering occasional respite. We all make this difficult journey a little more bearable, a little less frightening.

You and Julie didn't have that. Somehow, you just knew the best things for Timmy. I didn't appreciate then that you were also young (you seemed very old to me!). I remember Timmy's command to "PRAY!" when the oxygen wasn't enough. Our eyes met when he was dying. His gaze held me until it was clear that he was looking beyond anyone in the room.

The praying part of Timmy's lesson fell away from my life, replaced with clinical knowledge. Recently it's come back to me. After a very hard winter, with too many hours of work, a beeper that was never off, a spring that stood us up here in Maryland, and my family suffering from my frequent and unpredictable absences, I did finally come to recognize that prayer was missing. This past Sunday, in Meeting, when I remembered Timmy's lesson, I finally understood it and it became a part of me. It was as though I sat with Timmy last week, instead of 28 years ago.

I pronounced Linda [dead] two days ago. She left as easily and peacefully as Timmy did. Her story is in yesterday's [local paper].

Love,
Sue

*   *   *

It has been almost three decades since Timothy's death and I have had wonderful resources to process this part of my life. With so much distance, I can see some of the gifts that period in my life brought me. Now, each small child that crosses my path is the most precious creature in the universe. Over the years, I have learned how to give them my complete and undivided attention, cherishing each moment. Yesterday I spent a delightful half hour with a friend's three-year-old, her smiles filling the room with sunlight while she explored the rumbly sounds of the big Mother drum that still sits in my room. Sometimes, there is a sweet sadness afterward that I hold like a fresh-picked rose, smelling its essence long after I have put it down.

Now, with surgery very close, I had the answer that could speak to this biggest of all my fears. If, for my surgery, I could approximate to even the tiniest degree the prayerful loving community that had supported us through Tim's last two weeks, then perhaps Grendel's Mother would rest easy in her swamp and not disturb my recovery.

CHAPTER 17

Grendel's Mother Defeated

may my heart always be open to little
birds who are the secret of living
whatever they sing is better than to know
and if men should not hear them men are old

may my mind stroll about hungry
and fearless and thirsty and supple
and even if it's sunday may i be wrong
for whenever men are right they are not young

and may myself do nothing usefully
and love yourself so more than truly
there's never been quite such a fool who could fail
pulling all the sky over him with one smile
                                    —*E. E. Cummings*

Sunday, August 3, 2003

My heart valve surgery was only two days away. The hospital had scheduled the paperwork early in the morning a full day ahead of surgery, so to avoid Monday's commuter traffic Delia and I left home that evening, planning to stay in a motel near the hospital. As we drove, it was reassuring to have Delia chatting beside me. Soon, with the familiarity of the highway and drone of the engine, we grew silent and my mind began to drift.

Was it only five days before? Everything had seemed fine. Even though the doctors had been giving dire warnings, I had felt okay—perhaps a little more tired, a little less energetic, but nothing alarming. But that day Sierra had invited Delia and me to watch her play violin at a Celtic concert in a local park. We were late. Finding a parking place, we jumped out of the car, and strode rapidly across a huge mown field. Fifty paces from the car I was panting, out of breath. I paused. *Damn, this isn't right.* As I stood there gasping, I could feel the hot sun reach through the back of my shirt and begin to suck the first itchy sweat from my pores. I looked up. Fifty yards ahead was a stand of ancient oaks, their wide branches forming dark pools of cool shade. How I longed to be there. In a few moments I tried again. Thirty more paces and I had to bend over, hands on my knees, as though I had just run the hundred yard dash.

Delia said, "What's the matter Tom? This isn't like you."

"I think it's my valve. We'll have to go slower."

"This is getting serious, isn't it?"

"Yeah," I said, "Good thing the surgery is just a few days away. I don't think it could have waited any longer."

By slowing down we eventually reached the cool shade. There the going became easier and soon we were sitting in front of an outdoor bandstand, watching Sierra and her little group of fellow musicians. But all through the concert I was aware of how my body was now reinforcing my doctors' warnings: Get this leaking valve fixed or else!

My awareness returned to the drive to the hospital and Delia's reassuring presence next to me. She had been so helpful two days before when a large group of friends had come to our house to help in my final "rite of passage" toward surgery. How excited I had been. While Delia vacuumed and dusted everywhere, I gathered all our chairs and floor cushions from the rest of the house. Meanwhile, just outside my open window, flocks of birds were singing at the feeders and the warm August sun was encouraging Delia's flowers to put on their brightest colors for our guests. As a last step, we said some prayers and sprinkled tiny bits of cornmeal and tobacco around the room to recreate the sacred circle of my vision quest. If my prayers were answered, this sacred circle would continue to hold me through my stay in the hospital, just as it had on the mountain side two years before.

Despite the cheerful day, a coarse rasping of remaining fear had gnawed at the back of my brain. I was longing for safety, still unsure that I would survive. Yet from my experiences with Timothy, I knew that prayer and a caring community would help. The knighthood in the garden and having my friends anoint me from the vial of holy oil had been important beginnings, but today I wanted to create an even deeper ritual of preparation. Since ritual was one of Mary Ann's specialties, she would be leading us.

The first to arrive were three of my fellow Quakers. There was Allen's gruff "Thank you," as I lowered his stroke-ravaged body into my easy chair, his wife Rosalie hovering nearby. Then came Leoma's ancient Volvo sputtering its way up the street, followed by the sound of her walking sticks tapping their way down the stone path as she hobbled through the garden and finally collapsed on the couch. Leoma's my example of toughness under fire, one for whom the words "sufferer" or "patient-of-MS" do not apply. Involved in a dozen activities and on numerous committees, she manages to get everywhere with leg brace and hiking sticks, a smile and a good word for everyone.

I remembered Delia coming to stand with me as I greeted each person, and how she took my hand with a reassuring squeeze. A moment later three of her oldest friends arrived. They held her in a long embrace, then wandered off with her for a quiet chat.

When elderly Roger and his wife Peggy arrived, I took Roger's arm and led them to a comfortable place on the couch. Roger is one of my best buddies. A luminous bear of a man, he's one of the few people I can pour my soul into and feel completely safe.

A few moments later I was surprised and delighted to see my shamanic friend, Barbara, walk in the door. She lives so far away I hadn't bothered to invite her, but here she was with another friend, both giving me big smiles and hugs. I had met them a few years before at a two-week shamanic workshop, and we had remained friends ever since.

Turning back into the room I noticed Jim, my shy, silent walking companion, leaning against the far wall, arms crossed, watching. Sitting near him was my cello teacher, her bright yellow dress contrasting nicely with the dark green cushion under her. Looking at her and remembering our lessons, I could almost hear the rich tones of her instrument reverberating through the room.

Soon the space was filled beyond capacity: every chair, every cushion, every bit of floor space taken, so that the last arrivals were left standing near the door. When I finally sat down, I had to squeeze close to Barbara, so close that our shoulders and hips were mashed together and her musky perfume mingled with that of the ceremonial tobacco used in our prayer ties[24].

Ah, the prayer ties. So cheerful. While everyone was intent on making them, I scanned their faces, cementing each in my memory as companions for the long ordeal ahead. Soon there were dozens of little swatches of brightly colored cloth tied to long white strings, each holding a pinch of tobacco and a prayer—prayers for Delia or for me or for someone else in need. When everyone finished, and I tied the separate strands into one huge circle, I felt humbled and awed.

Through it all, Mary Ann stood at the big mother drum, eyes closed, her steady rhythm rumbling through the room like distant thunder, yet carrying the calm reassurance of a mother's heart beat.

*   *   *

As the traffic slowed to a crawl, I felt my left hand fumble with a small object hanging around my neck, my fingers rubbing it like a worry bead. Tala, that wise friend whose prescient timing always surprises me, had said, "Take this amulet, charge it with prayers, use it to bring those prayers with you into the operating room. There's no metal in it, only amber and cloth, so the surgeon should allow you to have it."

The morning of the gathering I had watched the amber make its slow way around the room, each person saying a silent prayer for me as they held it. When someone near the window held it up, it glowed in the sunlight, and in that golden glow I felt many more presences in the room: the knight and the young princess, my friends with the holy oil, the blessed souls who sat with Timothy in his last moments, the frog and insects of my vision quest, the third stone-mason building his cathedral to God—all those and more were here. So many people, so many prayers—more love in one small space than I had ever experienced, except perhaps with Timothy. I started to cry. As Barbara put her arm around me and held me close, I put my head on her shoulder and sobbed.

Later I realized that some of the depth of these feelings came because Delia and I see our friends only in small numbers: a few friends for a

---

[24]   See Appendix B—Making Prayer Ties

holiday meal; Sierra's family for chicken soup; a once-a-month shamanic circle or men's group; and on Sundays, a few friends at Quaker Meeting. Otherwise, nearly all my encounters are one-on-one.

I like it that way. I get to focus my attention fully on the friend who is with me, sharing our undivided attention for each other. Over time, I have developed a strong connection with each one. When I know they are coming, I eagerly await their arrival. When they go, we hug and I am reluctant to see them leave. Each time they come, the connection goes a little deeper until their lives are a part of my life, their friendship enriching me, making my life more meaningful, and giving it a rich inner glow that carries me forward and lightens my heart.

That day, however, was different. For the first time, all those dear friends were with me in one place and at one time. For a once-shy young man, this was a huge contradiction to the abandonment and loneliness of my childhood. In that room, sat my battalion of trusted soldiers, the ones that would defeat the monster, the "Grendel's Mother" of my fears. All morning I had collected images and feelings, placing each friend in my memory like snapshots in a picture album, gathering my army into the prayer ties and amulet for the march toward a successful surgery.

*   *   *

Late that evening we arrived at our destination and spent the night in a motel near the hospital. The next morning we drove to our appointment with hospital admissions where I spent a couple of hours completing page after page of forms. At lunch I could hardly eat, my stomach doing noisy flip-flops. Surgery wasn't until the following morning, so with the rest of the day free, we wandered through town, distracting ourselves with the sights. Late that afternoon, Carl showed up at our motel.

More than thirty-five years ago, Delia had met Carl in Nepal during a year's adventure traveling around the world. Carl and his friend, Peter, had been finishing their tour of duty in the Peace Corp. Delia and Peter fell in love, were married, and settled near Peter's home in Northern California. Eventually Carl moved from the East Coast to Davis, California where he became a university professor. Carl had remained a close friend even after Delia's divorce. Now, hearing of our crisis, Carl had driven down to be part of Delia's support team while I was in surgery.

That evening, Carl checked into our motel while we checked out, moving to the hospital's guest house. I was so glad that Carl had come. I knew that Delia would need support for the long ordeal ahead, and Carl's calm easy presence would be a balm and an anchor for her.

As instructed, I took a special shower with an iodine wash and scrubbed every inch of myself for the morning's surgery. I was wired—nervous about the surgery, curious about what the next morning would be like, fascinated with the iodine wash, so it took a while before I finally fell asleep.

The next morning, within a half-hour of our 4:30 wakeup call, we heard a knock on our door. A staff member was there to make sure I made my 5:30 a.m. appointment for surgical prep.

After signing more papers and taking a couple of pills, I was led to a small room where I was told to undress and lie on the table. In walked a huge man. With a serious, almost grim expression, he prepared to shave me from neck to foot. With slow careful strokes he began. Such strange thoughts: *What a bummer—he's removing what little manly chest hair I have.* Then: *Only women and swimmers shave their legs.* And later: *How strange it is to have a man shave my pubic hair and around my privates.* All through it, the big man kept a stern face and said nothing. Meanwhile, Delia and Carl stood beside me, admiring the man's skill, and trying to stay cheerful.

When he was done, the man handed me another package of iodine wash, aimed me toward the shower, and told me to scrub everywhere *very* thoroughly. Feeling like a skinned rabbit, I climbed into a surgical gown and did as I was told.

After the shower I again gowned, fingered the golden amulet around my neck, then lay face up on a waiting gurney. With the easy grace of long experience, a tall slender nurse slid an IV shunt into a vein on the back of my hand. As she started to roll me away, I grabbed Delia's hand for a quick squeeze and waved goodbye to Carl. Off we went. As we neared the doors to the sterile area, I closed my eyes and imagined the sound of my drum. Within a second or two I was with my most powerful lower-world teacher. "Come be with me in surgery," I pleaded. "Help me through this trial."

"I'll be with you, deep inside where I can protect you the most," she said. "Do not fear—all will be as it should be."

I thanked her, heaved a deep sigh of contentment, and opened my eyes. I was greeted by three or four surgical staff with welcoming smiles and encouraging words. We chatted.

In the blink of an eye, everything changed.

PART TWO

Purgatorio

Meanwhile we reached the mountain's foot; and there
we found so sheer a cliff, the nimblest legs
would not have served, unless they walked on air. . . .

My Guide exclaimed: "Now who is there to say
in which direction we may find some slope
up which one without wings may pick his way!"

To course over better waters the little bark of my
wit now lifts her sails . . .

Commedia (Purgatorio)
Dante Alighieri, 1265-1321
translator 1st 6 lines: *John Ciardi*
translator last 2 lines: *John D Sinclair*

CHAPTER 18

The Ascent Begins

I experienced no dreams, no restless sleep, no momentary wakefulness, no sense of time passing. I was in the operating room—blink—I was somewhere else. It was as though the hours between chatting with the operating room staff and coming to consciousness in what must have been the Intensive Care Unit had been stripped from the fabric of my universe.

Everything was different. It wasn't just the unfamiliar, dimly-lit room with no windows, nor the IV in my hand. It wasn't that I felt infinitely heavy, as though glued firmly to my bed. It wasn't even the pretty Thai nurse fussing with something at the foot of the bed. Rather, in some inexplicable way I had changed. Was it that modern medicine had worked its miracle on my heart? Perhaps. Was it deeper than that? My mind was too foggy to know. But though I could barely twitch a finger, I was ecstatic. I wanted to shout to the world that I had survived the surgery. I was *alive*.

I raised my hand a few inches from the bed. The nurse looked up, smiled, and gestured to someone. To my great relief, Delia moved into view. If I had had the energy, I would have wept for joy, but I just lay there.

"Welcome back, tough guy," she said as she gently squeezed my big toe. "We've been waiting for you to wake up." She turned to the nurse and I could hear her whisper, "He looks so tiny and frail!" Turning back to me, she said, "Wow, Your eyes are so big—such an intense blue. I've never seen them like this."

I tried to respond but something was blocking my throat. I felt thwarted. I longed to tell Delia everything: how all my preparations had worked, how comforted and protected I had felt in that last-minute journey to my shamanic teacher, and how I had felt so completely prepared! Frustrated, I gestured for pen and paper.

The nurse said something, but I couldn't understand her Thai accent. I gestured again. Finally she said, "I think he wants to write something," and went off to get a pen and pad. When she put them in my hands, I had just enough strength to write "Journey good!" I watched Delia try to decipher the pen scratches and . . .

Again time hiccupped—again I didn't exist.

A tiny window opened to my brain and I looked out through a dense haze of anesthesia. Two medical staff hovered over me. The doctor said, "We've been giving your body some time to recover, but now we're going to take out the breathing tube. It will be a bit uncomfortable but very quick. Here we go . . ." He reached toward my mouth, grasped something I couldn't see, and gave a long pull. For a second or two, there was an inner scraping and yanking, like a corrugated snake[25] rippling through the length of my chest, turning my throat and windpipe to liquid fire. I wanted to gag, choke and cough all at the same time. Before I could rise up to fight them off, it was all over, the sensation gone.

They watched me for a moment.

The earth turned in its orbit without me.

I was still lying on my back, but in a new place. I felt, rather than saw, soft green light coming from my left. I turned my head. The high branches of a tall leafy tree were just out of reach. *Oh, they've put me in a tree house.* But it was just a window and I was in an ordinary hospital room. On the wide sill below the window were spread all one hundred and fifty prayer ties, wound back and forth in long colorful strands. Next to them were Delia's purse, a bouquet of flowers, and a potted bonsai plant. It must have been evening because there was just enough light to see Delia sitting in a chair at the foot of the bed. I was so glad to see her I wanted to weep. "Hi" I croaked.

She looked up from her book. "Oh, you're awake. Welcome back again!" She got up, walked over to my bed and took my hand. She looked like an angel come to return me from the dead. I was so weak, lifting my hand took the greatest effort, lifting my head was like trying to lift a dump

---

[25]   The tube is actually very smooth.

truck—impossible. Luckily I had no desire to move, only to sleep and drift and sleep again.

Later, a nurse came in. As Delia stepped out of the way, the nurse reached below the edge of the bed and brought up a coil of tube full of pink liquid. She moved the coil in some mysterious fashion, making the fluid move from the bed toward what I imagined was some container below. She continued with a second tube.

"What are you doing?" I asked.

"I'm making sure the fluids in your chest are draining properly. I'm also measuring the amount of fluid to monitor the progress of your healing."

Footsteps woke me. My friend Leslie had arrived. I hadn't been sure how things would be during the first few nights—this was a big unknown. Would I be totally helpless? Would the nurses be responsive? Would I have some crisis with no one to help? (My abandonment fears had been on full alert, anticipating the worst.) Delia would be wonderful during the day, but she would need a good night's sleep to stay fresh and present, and for her own health. So I had hired Leslie to come spend the first night in my room.

That evening, after Delia left for her own bed, I lay there, my head on the pillow, the rumpled sheets under my hands, my body sunk deep into the mattress. In the night I woke to pain for the first time. It must have been kept under control all day, but now there was an intense ache centered in my middle back. Not wanting to wake Leslie, I pressed the call button. Within moments I heard, "Mr. Snell?" Pause. "Mr. Snell? What can we do for you?"

Disconcerted by the disembodied voice I took a moment to say, almost in a whisper, "I'm having some pain. Can someone help with that?"

"Sure. We'll be right there."

Luckily, Leslie didn't stir. In less than a minute a nurse was hovering nearby. As she handed me a pill, I asked, "Why's the pain in my back?"

"Your back's affected because the surgeon had to spread your ribs to get inside, and that disturbed where those ribs attach to your backbone." She said this as she held a cup and straw to my lips to wash down the pill.

"Oh," I said. *This is great*, I thought. *These people are on the ball*, and I drifted back to sleep.

Twice I woke when the nurse came to check my drainage tubes and IV. Each time I was reassured by the sight of my friend curled up on the cot. Then I would lie awake for awhile and listen to the sounds just outside my door.

Two years later, to gather material for this book, I used the shamanic process to journey back in time to the hospital. I wanted to see what might be under the anesthesia; what might have gone on in those blank spots where I hadn't seemed to exist. It wasn't so much that I wanted to "see" the physical details of the surgery, but rather to find out what my shamanic teachers might show me if I asked. So I lay down, put the blindfold over my eyes, and let the drum carry me into other worlds.

It's early morning. We're in the operating room watching the surgery. The prayers of my friends rise like benevolent ghosts from the amulet around my neck, and they, as well as my power animals and teachers, create a sacred circle of prayer and protection. Within this circle the surgeon has already opened my chest, exposing everything. *They've taken away the armor around my heart. How vulnerable I look*!

One of the teachers says, "Do you remember the journey you took with us to decide about Doctor Valve-a-Day, the one where he guided you through the great storm? Watch."

Superimposed over the scene in the operating room is a ghostly image of the rock-bound coast of Maine where I grew up. A complex maze of islands, inlets, rocky shoals and hidden ledges, it's a dangerous place for the sailor who doesn't know its waters. A single mistake and the unforgiving granite can rip the bottom out of any boat. Yet there, hovering over the operating table is the Egg Rock Lighthouse of my childhood. Visible by walking only a few hundred paces from our doorstep, its steady lamp has been as reliable as the sunrise. Her light and horn guide the local lobstermen through fog or dark, past the dangerous rocks and shoals, as they work their way homeward after the day's catch.

One of my teachers says, "To protect you from the hazards of surgery, we will send your soul far out to sea where it can ride out the storm in safety."

Suddenly I feel a jolt. *The surgeon has stopped my heart!*

*   *   *

I'm three. My mom has just tucked me in bed. With my window open to the soft summer air, I'm lulled to sleep by the distant sound of Egg Rock's fog horn.

I'm four and this is my favorite time of day. It's when Mom practices her piano. With crayons and a coloring book spread out on the floor in front of me, I listen to her fill the house with the genius of Chopin, Schumann, Brahms and Beethoven, her favorite composers.

I'm five. I smell mice—lots of them. Dad has just come home from work and an invisible cloud of animal musk swirls around him like a brown aura. All day he's been in the mouse room at the lab culling his research colonies. After supper my brothers and I get ready for bed. We each have separate rooms at the top of the stairs, so Dad sits outside in the hall weaving a magic web of stories to put us to sleep. I like the stories, but wish he were holding me in his lap instead of sitting in the hall.

I'm six. One afternoon after school, as I drift through the kitchen, I start to play with part of the old fashioned kerosene cook stove that stands against one wall. One of its special tools fascinates me. It's a long, springy iron rod that, if inserted into a hole at the side of the stove, will stick out horizontally. I adjust it just so, then pull downward and give it a sudden release. It bounces in a deliciously long and slowly decaying rhythm. As it bounces it gives off a boing, boing, boing sound that repeats faster and faster as the bounce and sound fade away. Spellbound, I'm repeating this over and over and over.

"WHAT THE DEVIL ARE YOU DOING!?"

My dad's sudden temper bursts like a bolt of white-hot lightning crackling out of a perfect blue and gentle sky. It crashes down so unexpectedly from high above that my body ducks in a violent and startled lurch. The ferociousness of it splits me asunder for a moment, like seeing pieces of myself in a cracked mirror. Then, just as suddenly, the raging sound is gone, snuffed out by a towering self control, the sky clear-blue again, my surroundings untouched. It's so quiet that I wonder, *did anything happen?* Yet my body still shakes, and deep inside the cracks remain.

I'm seven. My favorite hideout is the garage roof. I get there by shinnying up a Norway maple, working my way along a branch, then stepping gingerly onto the shingles. Today my friend Charlie has come too. He's brought three fish he's caught and gutted earlier in the day. "Let's lay them in the sun. If they dry, we can eat them." So we spread them out carefully, flesh exposed to the warm summer sun, and wait. Soon we're bored. Charlie says, "Let's play spook with old Mrs. Haymer."

The garage has been placed so its roof is only inches from Mrs. Haymer's roof, and just a few feet farther are the vent pipes that wind their way up from the bowels of her sewer. Tiptoeing across, we take turns bending over, our mouths a half inch from the pipe, making moans and wails that reverberate back in deliciously ghoulish echoes. Getting no response, we finally give up, climb down from our roof top, and go home to our respective suppers.

Charlie never comes into my house—few of my friends do. If I do bring a friend home, my mother manages our every moment. Intensely uncomfortable with the chaos of little boys, she hovers inches from us the whole time. As soon as I bring one in the door, she herds us into the kitchen in her fluttering way and sits us at the old table with, "Here's a checkerboard, dear. Why don't you both sit right here and play checkers?" Or, "Tell me everything about your day at school, every detail." Then she waits with an exasperatingly expectant face, wanting something neither of us knows how to give. I'm mortified and soon stop bringing anyone home.

The only visitors to the house are people my Dad invites: fellow scientists from work, or collaborators from what, to a small child, are exotic places—England or Czechoslovakia or Chile, places I only know about from my stamp collection or the globe that sits in my room. My mother polishes the good silver and prepares the dining-room table, while Dad brings home a bottle of sherry, or a little dry vermouth for Martinis or bourbon for Old Fashioneds. For an evening or two the house fills with talk of mouse genetics and cancer research, the H-2 locus[26] and inbred strains, congenic lines and the immunologic rejection of tissue grafts—nothing that a small boy can relate to.

Suddenly, the rumble of the weekly freight train that growls its slow deliberate way behind our California home, pulls me out of the journey. Frustrated, I wait for the floor to stop shaking and the train's roar to fade into the distance. Soon it's gone and the soothing rhythm of the drum draws me back into the journey.

"What's going on?" I ask one of my power animals.

"When the doctor stopped your heart, it's as though you had died," he replies. "I'm showing you your life as it would have flashed before you, were it not for the anesthesia. Watch, and do not interrupt again."

I'm eight and it's winter. As I do most school nights, I've followed Charlie home. We take off our snow clothes on his family's enclosed

---

[26]   H-2, the major histocompatibility complex of the mouse. It was for the discovery and understanding of this gene complex that my dad got the Nobel Prize.

porch, step inside, and turn on the radio. It's story hour. While Charlie's mother cooks in the nearby kitchen, Charlie and I lie in the middle of the living-room floor totally absorbed in the ongoing sagas of Tom Mix, The Lone Ranger, and Superman. Reluctantly, at five o'clock, I pull on my heavy coat and snow pants, thrust my feet into my warm boots and start home for supper.

In Down-East Maine, night comes early in winter. Many afternoons, when it's overcast or the moon has not yet risen, the lower part of my street can be pitch-black by five o'clock. Tonight it's started to snow, so when I step outside and leave the glow from Charlie's kitchen window, the only thing to guide me home is my memory of the way and a faint reflected sparkle from the blanket of white spread everywhere. Inching along, hands outstretched, feet feeling their way, my mind begins to play its familiar trick of hearing bogeymen and ghosts behind every bush. *Crack!* A branch snaps in the cold. *Creeeeeak!* The wind sways a nearby tree, rubbing two large branches together. *Woooooo!* The wind moans in the treetops. By the time I slip in our backdoor, my heart is pounding and my inner clothes are damp with sweat. Yet the next afternoon, there I am at Charlie's again, listening raptly, warmed by the easy acceptance of his parents, and repeating the scary journey home once more.

I love stories. If I'm not at Charlie's I'm at the town library. Like some lord's great keep, the library has a ten-foot-high, double front door covered in heavy leather and iron studs. Whenever I walk in past the librarian's desk to the central reading room, I always look up. High overhead, circling the room, is an ornate, iron-railed balcony holding more stories than a boy could ever hope to read. During the school year, when I'm not doing homework, I can ride the river with Tom and Huck, explore the jungle with Kipling's Mowgli, ride to a damsel's rescue with one of King Arthur's men, enter the archery contest with Robin Hood or follow the many adventures of Doctor Doolittle. The library is my refuge—the castle where my imagination thrives.

It's summer and I'm ten. Mother has gone out so Dad takes me to the lab for the afternoon. We go into the mouse room where he's been working. After demonstrating, he has me pick up one of the mice by its tail. He shows me how to set it on the table top and pull it ever so gently backwards so the little mouse is kept busy scratching its tiny nails against the smooth wood, trying to get a purchase and get away. Then, while still holding onto its tail with one hand, he uses his other to gently grasp the mouse at the neck, just behind its head. With a quick pull and squeeze it's dead, only a small bundle of skin and bone remaining, ready for the trash barrel at our feet.

"These are the ones we no longer need, and we must make space for new ones," he says. "You can help." So for the rest of the afternoon we cull the unneeded mice from his stock. Such mixed feelings—proud to help, yet repulsed. I hate killing, but for the next hours I fight my squeamishness and do as I'm told.

Later that week I go with Dad to the town's athletic field to watch him play on the lab's softball team. When it's his turn at bat and he steps up to the plate I think, *He's doing it all wrong!* Instead of the bat cocked back at shoulder height like everyone else, he's holding it almost directly overhead. Then the pitch comes. In one swift motion he brings the bat straight down. Miraculously it connects, and the ball sails out over the infield and directly to the center fielder. Reaching up for an easy out, the fielder's astonished when the ball slips out of his grasp. Three times Dad does it and three times the fielders flub the ball. Walking home I can't stop grinning, I'm so proud of my dad the softball player! It was only later that I understood that his unorthodox method placed such a tremendous spin on the ball that it was nearly impossible to catch.

I'm twelve. I'm in a big basement room at the YWCA, here for a dance class my parents insist that I take. It's a big room, almost square, and all the tables and chairs have been moved to one end, leaving a big open space. The girls are lined up against one wall, we boys against the other. We're to choose partners. But I want to crawl away and hide, to make an opening between the wallpaper and plaster so I can disappear into that thin and secret space, not to come out until everyone is gone. But I just stand there, frozen, my heart racing, with that look that a gazelle has when the cheetah is almost upon it. Finally there's only myself and one girl, and I'm rescued from having to choose.

Suddenly there are two hard jolts. Still in the journey, this rapid flood of childhood images is replaced by the opening scene in the operating room. The surgeon has finished his repair and jolted my heart to beating again. My teacher and power animals are still holding sacred space around the operating table. As before, the ghostly image of the coast of Maine is spread across the room, while Egg Rock Light hovers directly over my body. My power animals, together with Delia and all the friends who had risen from the amulet, reach out and touch the tip of the lighthouse tower, lighting its lamp. A dozen tightly focused beams shoot toward the horizon like arrows toward some distant target. One of the beams swings past a shadow far out at sea. It's my soul, sent off to safety at the start of surgery. The soul steps into the corridor of light, and, like a winter's child making the last snowy run of the day, slides down the beam and into my waiting body. The journey is over and I'm safe, back in my room at home.

*   *   *

In the morning, the gentle light that filtered through the treetop windows of my hospital room drew my attention to the prayer ties. *Ah, my friends are here.* It was as though half a dozen of them were sitting on the deep sill, swinging their legs like small children, and smiling. Their presence was so strong that I knew I wouldn't need Leslie again. All week, I had only to glance toward the window and they were there. With them nearby, my anxiety didn't have a chance.

There is something very elemental in having our friends close by, something out of our stone-age heritage where, when danger lurks, we feel protection in numbers. It's as though I had been wounded in the hunt, and my tribal group was standing watch at the mouth of the cave, protecting us all from the Saber-toothed Tiger lurking just outside.

After breakfast, the nurse introduced me to what I call "the torture device[27]," an eight-inch-high cylinder of clear plastic with a breathing tube attached. Inside the cylinder was a loose-fitting blue plunger. The goal was to exhale, then inhale long and steady through the tube, forcing the plunger upward, my breath holding it up as high and as long as I could. Torture may be too strong a word, but the discomfort began on the exhale and continued all through the longest inward breath I had ever tried. Coughing and sputtering I tried again. More coughs—more sputtering.

"Good," the nurse said. "This is what we want. It will keep you from getting pneumonia and strengthen your lungs. You should do this at least ten times, repeating it once an hour while you're awake."

At first I was discouraged—the plunger barely moved. But I knew that working this monster was one of the secrets to my recovery. Besides, I had

---

[27]   An incentive spirometer

little else to do. I wanted so much to return to my beloved woodland trails, hours and days wandering off the beaten path, drenched in nature. I knew I couldn't do that without strong lungs and a strong body. So, with Delia's encouragement, I kept at it, continuing even after I got home.

At noon, as the nurse elevated my bed for lunch, I noticed bruises around both my wrists. Alarmed, I quizzed the nurse. "Don't worry. There're okay. You got them during surgery. They strap your wrists and arms down to help open your chest. The bruises should go away in a day or two."

I immediately thought of the journey[28] I had done weeks before to help with my fear of the surgeon's knife. In the journey Hawk and I had looked down on my naked body stretched full length on a narrow altar. Lying face up, my arms had been stretched out and back, chest raised high, just as the nurse was describing. How had my power animal known this strange detail of the surgery? I certainly hadn't.

Early that afternoon I heard a knock at my hospital room door. "Mr. Snell, may I come in? I have something for you."

"Sure," I said, "What is it?"

In walked a buxom middle-age lady. "My, you've got quite a few friends—they've been sending you emails," and she handed me four sheets of paper.

"Thanks!" I grinned.

Weeks before, I had sent a blanket email to everyone that explained my situation and gave the address for the hospital's email web page. Now they were responding: one from my brother in Vermont, another from an old friend in Maine, a third and fourth from two friends in Maryland whom I hadn't seen in years.

As I read them, my feelings were so close to the surface that I found myself crying at the most mundane sentiments: "Hi Tom, just sending a little love your way. Dave" or "Get well soon, tough guy. Linda". Delia kept them within easy reach so, when I was awake with nothing else to do, I would read them again and again. By the third day I was getting quite a few, including emails from my grown kids, Chris and Sarah in Montana and Tamara in Los Angeles. Soon the email lady came twice a day, and each time her smile grew broader and the stack higher.

---

[28]   See chapter 10.

Late that afternoon I saw Sierra's parents, David and Jennifer, whispering outside my door. They glanced in, then looked away, unsure how to approach me. When Delia called to them, they finally stepped into the room. As they came closer and could see how weak and shrunken I was, Jennifer turned pale and David swallowed hard, his face dark with concern. Behind them was Sierra, half hidden by her mom, wanting to see her Gramps but not sure what to expect.

"Hi," I croaked in the strongest voice I could muster. "Looks like I'm still alive. Come on in." As all three came closer, I said, "Good news. The doctors were able to fix my valve. No replacement."

"Good," they chorused, as they gathered around the bed.

While Delia chatted with David and Jennifer, I encouraged Sierra to tell me about school and the sleepover she had done the night before. The more she talked, the more she relaxed. Soon she was her old self, chattering away, even talking about preparations for summer music camp where she would be playing her fiddle.

Then she asked, "Gramps, what's that thing around your head with the little tubes that go up your nose?"

"That's for oxygen. It gives my heart and chest lots of energy so they'll heal quickly."

"And what's that tube that goes from the back of your hand to the bottle hanging over you?"

"That's called an IV. It puts medicines directly into my body to help me get well. Here's something really cool," I said. "Hidden under my blankets are two tiny wires that go right through my skin and chest, all the way into my heart. The other ends are attached to a little box at the side of my bed. If my heart starts to beat too slow, the doctors can turn a dial to speed it up. Pretty amazing, huh?"

Sierra didn't answer—I could see that she was trying to absorb what I told her. Finally she said, "It's like turning up the sound on the car radio, isn't it? The farther you turn it, the stronger it gets."

"Yup," I said. "But they want to keep the volume just right. Too high and my heart won't heal properly, too low and it won't be good for me." I paused. "With all these wires and tubes I'm like the million-dollar bionic man."

My hospital care was excellent. Twice a day I was visited by two doctors, high priests of healing, medicine men and women who had substituted stethoscope for rattle, heart monitor for drum, X-ray for ayahuasca or peyote. At every waking and sleeping moment my heart was monitored by magic spells cast from a room far down the hall. Like an enchanted world, everything was managed for me. I was tired, but for a purpose. All the vitality normally used for everyday tasks was being diverted to millions of microscopic cells. Awakened by the injury, these cells had begun to divide and grow and divide again, stitching their way across the huge wound in my chest, creating strong new bone and skin. Eventually a thin white line would appear down the length of my sternum, the only remaining reminder of the surgery. Meanwhile, deep inside, similar cells, guided by the surgeon's skillful stitches, worked to repair my wounded heart.

The work of these cells reminded me of my mother. I could see her in the kitchen, her rocking chair creaking rhythmically as she sat late into the evening repairing our boyhood socks. Picking one up, she would drop in her darning egg, then pull the material around the egg, shaping the hole just so. Then, with just the right length of yarn, her needle would rise and fall, rise and fall, weaving the perfect patch that would last another month or two of hard play. Unlike my Mother, however, these cells are not quick. They work at their own pace, not mine. This wasn't something I could manage or control. My lesson for the next few weeks was to be patient and to trust their work and that of the doctors.

Ah, "trust". That was one of the keys. Thirty years before, trust had been central to our fight with Chris' and Tim's cancers. Through our long association with the doctors at Mass General, there had grown a strong bond of mutual friendship and trust that soon transcended the usual patient-doctor relationship.

But there had been a critical moment when we had been tempted to destroy that bond. In Tim's first eight-hour operation, one of the doctors had forgotten to use a tiny pillow between his head and the steel table. A blister formed that soon became a circular wound in his scalp nearly an inch and a half across. Because of radiation and chemotherapy, this wound never healed. Twice a day we had to remove the bandage, use sterile cotton and hydrogen peroxide to scrub away any puss and scabs, and then redress the wound. It was painful for all of us, and went on for fourteen months, right through the day he died.

About half way through our ordeal a neighbor said, "You know, this should never have happened. That doctor, the one who didn't put a pillow under your son's head, was incompetent. He's put you and Tim through a lot of pain and suffering. You should sue the bastard!"

We thought about it for a while. Certainly we could have used the money. Julie's and my combined salaries at The Meeting School consisted of room and board for our family plus $4200 a year. We had some help from our parents, but a little more could have gone a long way. By the usual standards, we would have been justified.

But our whole way of living would have been violated. As Quakers, Julie and I believe that there is something of God in each of us, that we are all trying to do our best, that the doctors are not infallible, but rather human beings like the rest of us, capable of mistakes, even grievous ones. Trust works both ways—the one who is trustworthy, and the one who trusts in them, their skills, their honesty, their integrity. Breaking that bond of trust by turning the doctor's mistake into a struggle for justice or revenge, finding who's "at fault" and making them pay for their mistake, would have destroyed too much. Here are just four examples.

It's the middle of the night and I'm keeping watch inches from Tim's bed. We're in Intensive Care. He's just had another eight-hour operation on his lungs and it's my turn to sit with him. There are nearly a dozen other children here, most in critical condition, but I'm the only parent. What a priceless gift: that the doctors would trust us enough that one of us could be at Tim's side through the long hours in Intensive Care, within instant reach should he need us. Twice in the night a nurse steps in to tend to another patient and I immediately leave until she is done. Then I return to Tim's bedside to keep watch.

Julie and I are in the radiation specialist's office, discussing Tim's progress. With two weeks of radiation left, we let slip that the daily trips from home to Boston, a one-hundred and thirty mile round-trip, have been taxing.

Doctor Linggood says, "Don't you have a place to stay here in Boston for the week—a hotel or something?"

"No," I say, "they're too expensive. But we do okay. The trip's not that bad."

"Well, you should have a place to stay. I have an apartment near the hospital. You could stay there."

"Doctor Linggood," Julie replies. "That's very generous of you. Thank you, but we can't. We have teaching responsibilities at home, and our other children need us after school, especially now. We'll be all right."

"Okay, but if you change your mind, let me know."

We never did take the doctor up on her kind offer, but her generosity had a huge impact on us. Over the ensuing years, whenever we thought of Mass General, we found ourselves coming back to that moment with gratitude.

It's Tim's last visit to Mass General. While the doctors examine him, Julie fills out the admittance forms, then goes to find his room. A few minutes later she hears a knock at Tim's door. When she opens it, she sees Doctor Kim, Tim's surgeon. He just stands there, mute. Looking closer she sees that he's crying. No words are necessary. She draws him into the room, puts her arms around him and they both cry for a while before he tells her the bad news.

It's Tim's memorial service, just three weeks after his death. As I step into the room where the service will be held, I notice that the place is packed. I scan the room to see who is here and notice two faces near the back that seem familiar. For a long moment I stare; then I recognize them. It's Jane and Lydia, two of the nurses who had taken care of Timothy. I fight back tears. Not only were they warm and caring in the hospital, but now they've taken time out of their busy day to make the four-hour round trip from Boston to say goodbye.

I'm convinced that things like this don't happen when you enter the adversarial world of the legal system, pitting one side against the other, forcing people to keep their distance, making them the enemy rather than your friend. A legal battle would have put them on their guard, made them cautious so they would not risk anything that might be misconstrued. We would have become, not the patient's parents but the enemy, the ones who could ruin their reputations, or at least drive up their insurance costs. We wanted the doctors on our side. We wanted them relaxed and caring, wanted all their hearts and minds and souls fighting for our son.

Of course money from a settlement would have helped, and there are unjust situations where fighting the good fight is essential, but on my personal spiritual balance sheet, cash is a very poor and light-weight gift against love and compassion and kindness. If I had to choose, I would far rather be wrapped in the arms of a strong community of friends who love and cherish me and my family, than have a million dollars.

Now, thirty years later, it was my turn to lie immobile. Rather than letting my energies be siphoned away by suspicion, mistrust, or doubt, I wanted all my vitality to go to those healing cells. Everything: Christopher,

Timothy, my power animals, and the prayers of all my friends, had been preparing me. Now it was time to relax into that inner place where I could trust that all would be okay.

On the second or third morning, after a doctor had removed most of the tubes and pipes scattered throughout my body, a nurse announced, "It's time to start walking Mr. Snell. I'm here to help."

At first it was just to the bathroom. With the nurse supporting me, I barely managed to shuffle the eight feet there, turn, and shuffle back. When I collapsed onto the bed, it felt as though I had done a solo climb of Everest without oxygen.

"We want you up and walking twice a day, so I'll be back again this afternoon."

Just before dinner, with her strong arm again around my waist, we went out the door and fifteen feet down the hall before returning. Soon I began to look forward to our walks.

But things still weren't right. My resting heart rate continued to dip too low, down to thirty-five to forty beats per minute, and it was skipping beats. Twice a day the doctors would hover over me, muttering mysterious incantations, their hands fluttering over the pacemaker dials, their heads shaking like shamans' rattles. No matter what they did, my heart, like a sullen and wounded teenager, continued to misbehave. Sometimes in the night I would wake with the alarming sensation that I had not been breathing. I would gasp for air, then force my chest to work, breathing in oxygen as though only my will would keep me alive. Then I would lie there, intensely conscious of the vital necessity of each breath until the near panic would leave and I would drift off to sleep again.

It was at times like these that I was grateful that, despite my request, the surgeon had decided not to do the Maze Procedure. I would still have to endure the atrial fibrillation and take blood thinner, probably for the rest of my life, but the extra stress of the procedure could very well have been more than my body could handle.

One morning the doctor suggested a blood transfusion. "We didn't need to use any extra blood for your surgery, but now we think a couple of pints could help. But it's up to you. There's some risk, so the choice is yours." After detailing the risks, he said, "Would you like the transfusion?"

I paused, but just for a moment. If there was even the slightest chance this would help, I wanted it. So I said, "Sure. Especially if you think it might make a difference."

And it did. Within a very brief time I could feel a small but significant change. My nighttime breathing came easier, and I felt significantly stronger. By the seventh day I was pacing the corridors like a caged tiger, doing as many as four laps around the heart wing before returning to my bed. A day later my heart became stable enough that the doctor could pull the temporary pacemaker wires from my chest, and on day nine, they pronounced me well enough to go home.

CHAPTER 19

Home at Last

A CUSHION FOR YOUR HEAD

Just sit there right now
Don't do a thing
Just rest.

For your separation from God
From love,

Is the hardest work
In this
World.

Let me bring you trays of food
And something
That you like to
Drink.

You can use my soft words
As a cushion
For your
Head.

—*Hafiz*, 14th century Persian poet
Translator *Daniel Ladinsky*

T hose nine days in the hospital had seemed an eternity, but finally, on a lovely mid-August morning, one of Delia's friends arrived to drive us home. As the nurse wheeled me to the hospital's front door, she handed me a tiny rectangular pillow. "Take this heart pillow home with you," she said. "Hold it to your chest. The pressure of the pillow will help with the discomfort, especially while riding in the car." With the two women chatting in the front seat, I sat in the back, holding the pillow to my chest like a child hugging his favorite teddy bear.

As I dozed I thought how lucky I was. I had survived the surgery; my heart had been repaired; and I had Delia, who had sat at my bedside through the whole ordeal. Now that I was going home, things would soon be back to normal.

Early the next morning, following doctor's orders, I stepped outdoors to walk. As was my habit, I turned left. But today, the slight upward slope from the bottom of our street to the house seemed daunting. *This will be too much. The way I'm feeling, I'll never make it back up the hill*! It was as though, overnight, the street had become a formidable mountain trail.

I was shocked. Fifteen years before, when I had lived in Maryland, I had risen at five each morning, slipped on my jogging shorts, and stepped out the door to run. At five o'clock the countryside had cooled from the fierce heat and humidity of the previous day, so, with the bright spot of my flashlight beam bounding down the path ahead, I would follow it for an exhilarating five mile run, returning forty minutes later for breakfast and the commute to work. Now I couldn't even walk this gentle slope. So I turned the other way, where the street is flat and ambled a slow fifty yards before returning home. Exhausted, I slipped into my easy chair and fell asleep.

I decided it was time for the Snell cure. Whenever I had gotten the flu, I had bought a cheap mystery novel, taken vitamin C, rented a few videos, and gone to bed. Within three or four days I would be much better, well on my way to recovery. It was time to do that again. So when I wasn't walking or breathing through the torture device, I would curl up in my easy chair, heart pillow clasped to my chest to ease the discomfort, and read my mystery novel. Soon the haze of the pain meds would take over and I would fall asleep. But as more and more time went by with little progress, I could see that this was going to be much more than a mild case of the flu.

Meanwhile, Delia took care of the household and kept me well fed. Despite the limits to her driving (local streets within three or four miles of home) she ran all the errands and took me to endless appointments. I washed the dishes and helped with grocery shopping, browsing the shelves for the smaller, light-weight items. When Sierra came to visit I would read a few pages to her, then drift off mid-sentence, only to jerk awake from the sound of my own snoring and continue.

Of course there were the pills! What had once been only a multi-vitamin and an occasional aspirin now became a whole pharmacy filling my bureau drawer. There were pills for cholesterol, pills for blood pressure, pills for atrial fibrillation, and pills for pain. There were so many it was downright confusing. Which three came before breakfast? How many blood-thinner pills was I supposed to take on Wednesday? How many on Thursday? Had I taken this evening's pills ten minutes ago, or was the mental fog of the pain meds confusing me with the day before?

So Delia bought me seven small boxes, each with multiple compartments. Every week I counted out the requirements for each hour of each day. At each appointed hour I would open a compartment and take the pills. If there were none there, then I had already taken them. For my drug-addled brain, this was much easier.

Still, I hated taking them. I didn't like the side affects and the very idea of being on medications made me feel even sicker and older than I was. What was worse, it looked as though I would be taking most of these pills for the rest of my life. At least I could stop taking the Vicodin and Tylenol once the pain was gone.

I didn't like the pain, but I was more afraid of addiction, so I followed the dosage requirements and kept careful records of how much I had taken and when. As my back healed, I slowly tapered the dosage away from the stronger drug and onto Tylenol, finally leaving that behind as well. After the first two or three weeks, I vowed that I would also find a way to stop taking most of the other medications.

But it wasn't time for that yet. My heart still had problems. All through the day I could feel it skipping beats, and every so often, for no apparent reason, it would start to race, accelerating from a normal seventy beats-per-minute to one-sixty, one-seventy, or even one-hundred-and-eighty beats-per-minute. Bam, bam, bam, bam it would go, like a frantic mouse trying to slam its way out of a cage. Sometimes it would last only a minute or two, sometimes for a couple of hours. This wasn't new. The atrial fibrillation had started a few months before surgery, but even though I knew it wasn't fatal, and that I had medications to keep it under control, it always alarmed me.

Even though I was slowly growing stronger and my head was clearing, I still wasn't allowed to drive or lift. With so little to do at home, it was hard to be patient and wait for the natural process of recovery. The long hours of inactivity began to annoy me, and I became irritable. One afternoon, after I was particularly grumpy with Delia, I remembered another time when I had not been patient.

*   *   *

After Timothy's death, Julie and I had worked hard to return to some semblance of a normal life. A few months after he died I spent two weeks in New Jersey getting help. For six hours a day, with the encouragement of two counselors, I cradled a weighted cushion in my arms as a make-believe-Timothy and sobbed my heart out. A year later I did it again, this time in Seattle. This was a potent resource and restored much of my old spirit.

Julie, on the other hand, stopped using co-counseling and tried other things. From my impatient perspective, she progressed much too slowly. I think that if I had been patient, the cracks in our marriage might have healed and our love might have survived, maybe grown even stronger. But I was not patient. Tim's death had altered the landscape of our marriage and I couldn't adjust. So the cracks grew wider. These stress fractures, like the tiny hairline cracks that can appear in a fine porcelain cup, widened and deepened, until the cup that held the essence of our marriage finally shattered in divorce eight years later. I paid for my impatience with estrangement from my family and ten lonely years.

Thinking of fragile porcelain, I was reminded of my Mother's heirloom teacups which she displayed in the cabinet Dad made for her. I was nine the year he made it. Each day, when he came home from work, we would go to the tiny room behind the kitchen where he kept his tools. While he worked, I watched. Rather than use plywood or veneer, he did it the old way with rosewood planks, hand-planing the edge of each board so they could all be glued and clamped to form a back, a side, or a deep shelf. He would slide his thumb down the edge to test its flatness, then stroke it with the plane, repeating again and again until it felt just right. By the time we stopped for supper, the floor was littered with curled shavings, and the smell of rosewood filled the little room. It was slow tedious work, but the final result was a labor of love that stood in the corner of my parent's kitchen for the next fifty years.

After our parents died, my brother and I could not afford to keep the house, so we sold it and auctioned the contents, including the china cabinet. For the next two years, each time I returned to Maine, I couldn't turn down our street, afraid that I would be overcome with sadness and shame—sadness for the loss of a home that held so many memories, and shame that we were forced to sell, not just a building, but what felt like the very cradle and soul of our family.

Now, with the surgery done, I hoped that the memory of Dad's slow, crafted patience might help me find a similar patience that would put my grumpy irritation to rest and help me heal.

At the end of six weeks a friend drove me north to see the surgeon for the first time since the operation. After a brief exam the surgeon said, "Your heart is still skipping beats and showing signs of atrial fibrillation. Those are things your cardiologist can monitor. Otherwise, everything looks good. Your heart and chest have healed from the surgery so I'm going to let you drive, and there are no longer any restrictions on lifting."

Despite the surgeon's good news, my recovery still seemed slow. On my next visit to the cardiologist he said, "The local hospital has a good rehab program for heart patients. I want you there, especially since we did a bypass for that one occluded artery. The rehab nurses will help with both exercise and diet."

By the second week I was enjoying my hours in rehab. The nurses were friendly, I was getting positive strokes for my efforts, and I could see measurable progress. On the nurse's recommendation I bought a portable heart-rate monitor to wear during my beach walks.

All this began to pay off. The more I went to rehab and the more I walked, the farther and faster I was able to go, until I was doing forty minutes a day at a pretty good clip. But it still wasn't enough. Even the smallest rise in the path would leave me panting, and my upper body had become fat and flabby. It was so bad I could feel the heavy flesh on my chest and belly bounce with each step, like a thirty pound, loose-fitting jacket of Jell-o, jiggling and quaking to its own rhythm. It was embarrassing.

So when the rehab program ended I joined the local gym. Perhaps some upper body work with weights and machines would help. But this would not be easy. The last time I had joined a gym I had quit after a few weeks, bored with the monotony of the routine. This time I was more determined, so I decided to ask for help.

When I told the gym's fitness expert about my operation, he cautioned me to start with a very light load, much lighter than I would have chosen. "With these machines you can add or subtract as little as one pound. Just add a pound or so every time or two that you come in. That way you can build up slowly without hurting your chest or inflaming any tendons or muscles. Take this card. It lists each machine down one side and dates across the top. Use it to record the weights you use and to track your progress."

Keeping records like this reminded me of Dad's garden records. Maine winters give a short growing season, so in March, while there's still snow on the garden and winter in the air, Dad would retrieve his handmade miniature greenhouse from the garage and climb the ladder to the second floor. There he would set its frame on deep brackets mounted just outside the wide upstairs bay-window. Inside the house he would raise the two sashes, seal the frame tight against the window's edge, and install his seed trays. Some seeds would be planted immediately, others later. For each seed type Dad consulted his records: When would the snow be gone? How long from placing this seed in the soil until its seedling was ready to transplant? When would the outdoor soil and air be just right to move each one to the garden? How had these seeds done last year? The year before? Ten years before that?

Warmed by the heat of the house and illuminated by the southern sun, his little seedlings would thrive, while just outside, the occasional spring storm would wake us to a fairyland of ice blanketing the trees and sparkling like a million diamonds in the morning sun. Finally, when the last of the ice had melted and his records showed that the time was right, he would transplant the mature seedlings into the garden. Within two or three weeks we would be the first in town to sit down to fresh picked greens. Within a few more weeks there would be peas or beans, carrots or beets on the table, and by midsummer it was sweet corn picked at five o'clock for dinner at six. What a culinary delight after a winter of stale, withered food trucked thousands of miles before reaching our table. Dad's careful records of snow dates, air and soil temperatures, and planting times kept over many years made this all possible.

This inspired me to keep thorough records at the gym. At first the weights seemed too easy. But, as the days and weeks went by and I slowly increased the load specific to each machine, it became more challenging. At times I would have to plateau at a given weight, but after a week or two I found that I could again move upward. Week after week I persisted. Ever so slowly firm muscle began to replace loose flab. Occasionally I would look back through the records, notice the progress I had made, and reward myself with a smile.

CHAPTER 20

The Fog and the Hawk

Under the Sill
Sometimes a
slow
malaise
seeps into the house. It
sighs under the sill,
hissing into the room like brain-choking
smoke.

Its grey mist
drifts over my couch,
whispers round the
stacks of unread
books, then
sifts a muffling layer of
dust over my carefully arranged clutter before
slipping into my bed.

Cuddling close,
its long seductive kiss
obscures the vital promise
that awaits me just outside my window.

—Tom Snell

O ne morning in mid-October, I woke to a dark and dismal day. For four days there had been a heavy overcast and steady drizzle. As I stepped to the car for the short drive to the beach, I turned up my collar against the cold and hunched over to keep the heavy drip from the trees off my glasses.

Instead of the beach, I tried the staircase to the top of the cliff that runs for miles up and down the coast as a sentinel between land and sea. The previous year, long before surgery, I had walked the full eight stories to the top once a week with my friend, Bill. Again and again we climbed, pushing ourselves a little more each week until finally, by late winter, we could do the full eight stories ten times in forty minutes. But this day was different. Today I could barely get halfway up before I was forced to retreat to the beach path, gasping for breath. Despite all my patience and nearly three months of hard work, I was becoming discouraged.

Surgery had disrupted much of my life. I had stopped seeing clients in my shamanic practice, I didn't have the energy for many social contacts, nor for the plays and concerts I had once enjoyed. In fact, surgery had curtailed much of my life. What little energy I had, had gone to preparation and recovery.

Now with the surgery over, I had not found anything to replace the adrenaline rush of crisis, nor the high of my friends' concern and attention, nor the sharp focus that glimpsing the veil had brought to my life. As I walked I thought, *Life's become so ordinary and I'm so bored with it all. I'm bored with the gym, bored with walking, bored with all this effort to get well. Am I ever going to recover?*

Where are my friends? Why aren't they calling? Is it because they think I've gotten through the crisis? And look how indolent I've become. For the past two weeks I've hardly left the Lazy-Boy chair in my room. I don't want to admit it, but part of me likes being a couch potato. Then another inner voice said, *Be careful. This is the route to heart attack and an early death. Wake up!*

I didn't like being dispirited, but the blahs persisted and I didn't know what to do about it. What had my nurse friends said? "Watch out. It's easy to get depressed after major surgery. Lots of people do."

The following Friday, Mary Ann arrived for our once-a-week morning of shamanic journeys. After lighting my altar candle, she glanced out the window and exclaimed, "Tom, look at the hawk!" In the middle of the garden path, not twenty feet away, stood a sparrow hawk[29], looking in our direction.

"Don't move," I whispered. "Let's see what happens." Hardly breathing, we watched the fierce little bird as he cocked his head first one way, then the other, scanning the garden. Could he see us behind the glass?

For what seemed like minutes the bird just stood there. Then, as though wanting to make sure we saw him, he took a few hops up the path, paused, then a few more, until he was only ten feet away.

"I've never been this close to a hawk," I said.

"Tom, since Hawk is one of your power animals, do you think this has some special significance?" Before I could answer, the hawk, with two quick wing beats, hopped onto the edge of the bird bath. Looking first one way, then the other, he dipped his head to drink.

"Yeah, maybe he's got something to tell me."

At that very moment the bird lifted into the air and disappeared over the trees to the north.

Starting out on an errand two days later, I backed my car out of our driveway and turned to go down the street. Before I could start forward, I was greeted by an amazing sight. Two feet off the road and forty feet in front of me was a Mourning Dove flying straight toward me. Ten feet behind her was the sparrow hawk in full acceleration. The dove's desperation was driving her forward at a furious clip, every muscle and feather tuned for escape. In a moment the dove whisked past my rolled up window and a second later the hawk followed, his left wing mere inches from the glass.

My whole body hummed with excitement. I wanted to reach out and touch the hawk as he passed. I wanted to feel the muscled eagerness of the chase and to borrow a little of his fierce purpose. I turned my head to look behind me. All the way up the street the birds continued their wild passage with no visible change in the gap between them. Seconds later they disappeared in the distance, the outcome unknown.

The moment I got back from the errand, I decided I had to act. I had been able to do something about my fears before surgery. Could I name this new beast, and through naming it, help resolve my doldrums?

---

[29] Now called American Kestrel, a member of the falcon family.

I pulled out my trusty journal and began to write. The first thing to appear was a description of my lethargy that eventually became the poem that opens this chapter. But as I continued I soon found myself drawn back thirty years to the period shortly after Timothy's death. For weeks I had been grieving, shedding buckets of tears and filling whole waste baskets with soggy Kleenex. One morning I woke to realize that part of my despondency had nothing to do with grief for Timothy. This was a different kind of loss. Tim's illness had brought my life into sharp focus. There was only: get Tim well, be with him when he needs me, and make sure the other kids are okay. Nothing else mattered. I had reorganized my job, my priorities and all my activities to make this possible. After he died, all that vanished leaving a huge hole.

Now, with my surgery a success and survival no longer an issue, a similar hole had appeared. My identity, that of someone facing a life-or-death crisis, was gone. I missed the adrenalin rush, the fierce drive to survive, and all the extra attention from my friends. As a retired person I had no job and no small children to keep me busy. Delia was healthy and involved in her own activities, but I was adrift.

Then I had another scary thought: *I've got to be careful. I miss this intensity and attention so much that, without knowing it, I might generate some new crisis just to get it all back!*

Clearly I had to do something. So much had changed I wasn't sure I could go back to the way things had been, but the way forward was shrouded in fog. What should I do?

PART THREE

Paradiso

. . . as much of the holy kingdom
as I could store as treasure in my mind
shall now become the subject of my song.

Comedia (Paradiso)
Dante Alighieri, 1265-1321
Translators Robert and Jean Hollander

CHAPTER 21

So Many Gifts

SO MANY GIFTS

There are so many gifts
Still unopened from your birthday,
There are so many hand-crafted presents
That have been sent to you by God.

The Beloved does not mind repeating,
"Everything I have is also yours."

Please forgive Hafiz and the Friend
If we break into a sweet laughter
When your heart complains of being thirsty
When ages ago
Every cell in your soul
Capsized forever
Into this infinite golden sea.

Indeed,
A lover's pain is like holding one's breath
Too long
In the middle of a vital performance,
In the middle of one of Creation's favorite
Songs.

Indeed, a lover's pain is this sleeping,
This sleeping,
When God just rolled over and gave you
Such a big good-morning kiss!

There are so many gifts, my dear,
Still unopened from your birthday.
O, there are so many hand-crafted presents
That have been sent to your life
From God.

—*Hafiz*, 14th century Persian poet
Translator *Daniel Ladinsky*

E arly the next Saturday morning Delia and I drove to the nearby
farmers' market for our week's supply of fruits and vegetables.
Between the second and third stalls we stopped to chat with Delia's friend
Sally. When Sally heard of my struggles with the grey blahs, she said, "I
spend fifteen minutes each morning being grateful—for my friends, for
my good fortune and for this beautiful place where we live. I always come
away feeling refreshed. Why don't you try it?"

"You're the second person who has mentioned gratitude recently," I
replied. "When I was in rehab, one of the nurses talked about it. What did
she say? Something about how gratitude is good for healing?"

As I headed toward our favorite fruit stand I remembered how, in the
hospital, I had been moved to tears by the smallest kindnesses. I had felt
so utterly grateful then. Could I bring back just a little of that feeling now?
I thought of Delia and how steadfast she had been. If I closed my eyes, I
could see her seated in the easy chair at the foot of my bed, reading her
novel and glancing up from time to time to see if I was okay. All through
each day she'd been there. If I slept, she read her novel. If I was awake, we
might chat a little. Once in a while she would walk the halls, or step out
with a friend for lunch, but soon she would be back, keeping me company,
never more than a few steps from my bedside.

After I got home, I tried again. I thought of Mary Ann and our shared
weekly journeys, of long talks with my buddies Joe and Bill, and of all
the friends who had come to the gathering just before surgery. I thought of

my friendship with Tala, and of all the wonderful people I knew through shamanism. The more I dwelt on these memories, the better I felt.

Then I remembered a trip to Maine two years before. My brother, Roy, and I had spent an afternoon biking the old carriage roads that wind their way through Acadia National Park. After an extended uphill stretch we stopped to rest, leaned our bikes against a tree at the side of the gravel road, and found a patch of wild blueberries hidden behind some nearby bushes.

As we picked, I began to tell him about Sierra, about the games we played and our shared love for the Harry Potter books. I went on and on, telling story after story, reveling in the memories of my friendship with this little girl who had made such a difference in my life. The more I spoke, the more animated I became. Suddenly I stopped mid-sentence, a look of surprise on my face.

Roy looked up. "What is it? What's going on?"

"I've just realized that I'm not just telling you about Sierra. I mean that's okay, and I'm glad to share her with you. What's really happening, however, is that even though she's three thousand miles from here, sharing her with you brings her close, almost as though she's right here eating berries with us. Sierra gives me an excuse to play and be silly. She makes me feel good. Through telling you, I'm reliving these experiences so I can feel those good feelings again."

Was this what gratitude did?

The next morning I strapped on the heart monitor and drove to the beach for my daily walk. The air was still damp from the morning fog, and just outside the breakers, a half dozen pelicans were diving for breakfast. Soon the walk and the waves became hypnotic. As I thought of Sally's words, I became intensely aware of my body, how easily my legs moved, how effortlessly they now carried me down the path. What a miracle to be alive!

Then I thought of the surgeon and his operating room staff and how grateful I was for their dedication and skill. Where had those skills come from? Less than sixty years ago the heart lung machine had not yet been invented, making open-heart surgery impossible. Much farther back we knew little of the workings of the human body, nothing of plastics, little of the sophisticated alloys that go into a modern surgeon's tools. Farther back, steel had not yet been invented, and earlier still, flint and obsidian were mankind's only cutting edges. How far we have come! My survival depended, not just on these wonderful people in the operating room, but on millions of individuals down through the generations, each of whom had discovered one or more steps toward today's final result, my return to health. How blessed I was to be born into this period in history.

Soon I grew eager for my walks. Where I had only seen ocean and sand before, I now saw miracle. As I watched the pelicans and gulls soar against a clear blue sky I thought, *How amazing to be able to see this exquisite view.* All my biology training from forty years before would come rushing back, and I would be reminded that none of this would be possible without the miracle of human vision. How do our bodies know how to make something as complex and specialized as the human eye? From the thousands of ever-so-tiny transparent cells that make the lens, to the millions of rods and cones that translate the light from pelican, sand, and sky into electrochemical impulses, the eye is a wondrous organ. These impulses then zip down the optic nerve to the brain where the image is processed far more quickly than a computer, providing instant recognition of people, dogs, pelicans and waves. But it doesn't stop there. The nerve cells in the brain then interpret the scene. Is it dangerous? Is it safe? I know the answer so quickly the thought never rises to awareness. Today my brain signals, "Notice how beautiful it is. I've sent 'good feeling' signals to your body so you can feel pleasure when you look. Bask in the view. Wake up to how good it feels."

Then I would be reminded of my heart, that intricate structure of muscle, valves, and pipes. It's tens of thousands of cells work in near-perfect cooperation to pump blood to and from all parts of my body and does so without ever stopping to rest. It starts from before birth and goes until the day I die. Yet it's *just* cells. Both my heart and my eyes are *just* cells—nothing more than tiny bags of chemicals and water. But what wondrous little packages! Somehow, from the uniting of one egg and one sperm sixty-four years ago at my conception, grew the cells that form these intricate organs. How did these two primordial cells know how to build eyes and heart and brain, things of such astounding complexity and perfection?

I know that very smart people have spent lifetimes searching for answers: the complexity of DNA, billions of years of evolution, God, Intelligent Design. But the more I thought about it, the more I realized none of these seemed satisfying. Instead, I found that I preferred no answer. Answers brought a closure to my experience, an "I've got the answer so I don't need to think about it any more" attitude. That seemed to shrink the miracle, to shrivel my amazement, to take away the awe. So I began to ignore the answers so I could revel in the mystery. Sally's words were working their magic. Things I had taken for granted my whole life were revealing themselves as the miracles they truly were.

Now that I was getting high on gratitude and my walking had progressed to where those natural spirit-lifters, the endorphins, were kicking in, work at the gym became easier. All the record keeping and gradual increase in effort was paying off. Where I had started at an easy thirty pounds I could now lift one-hundred and fifteen, ten pounds had now become forty-five. Firm muscle was replacing flab and friends were beginning to comment on how much younger I looked.

Despite all this progress, my heart continued to have brief bouts of rapid racing, whamming around in my chest for a few minutes, telling me that the atrial fibrillation (AF) had not gone away.

The racing wasn't so bad—it was the blood thinner that I detested. It was a risky medication that required constant surveillance and adjustment at the clinic, and because it was so sensitive to vitamin K in green vegetables, forced me to monitor every bite. At each visit to my cardiologist, I would moan, "I hate the blood thinner. I want to get off the blood thinner."

And every time he would say, "Not while the atrial fibrillation keeps happening. Without it you could have a stroke."

The whole thing was a royal pain. Except for another major operation there was no way to stop the AF, but I was desperate for a solution.

Then I remembered a painful knee that had appeared for no apparent reason. The doctors had muttered over me, the rehab nurse had tried his incantations, but there had been little progress. One night I woke at 3:00 am, my knee throbbing. I tossed and turned for what seemed like hours. Finally, rolling onto my right side, I noticed that from knee to foot the problem leg was not touching the bed. Suddenly it came to me: it was the new mattress!

I got up, rolled three towels into long cylinders, and stuffed them under the bottom edge of the mattress. I lay down. Now the mattress supported my whole leg. The throbbing was gone! Over the next few weeks my knee steadily improved.

Was there something like this causing the atrial fibrillation? Something I could fix? The AF had started a few months before we discovered the leak in my mitral valve. Was there anything I started doing then that I hadn't been doing before? Nothing came to mind, but I kept at it.

Then one afternoon while reading to Sierra, I noticed that two of my fingers were itching. I looked closer. Were those rough spots eczema? This wasn't the first time I'd scratched. These spots had been itchy many times over the last year. I just hadn't noticed. It was like the allergies of my childhood, a reaction to chocolate and peanuts that had made my fingers itch so much that I would scratch them raw. For years peanuts and chocolate had been forbidden. By college I had outgrown the allergies, and soon forgot them.

Was I allergic to something again? And if there was something, had I started eating it back when the AF started?

A year before the surgery Delia and I had attended a class on seed sprouting. We brought home the recipe for a deliciously satisfying blender concoction that used fresh fruit, yogurt, sunflower seeds, and almonds. It was so good we began drinking it every morning. A few weeks later, one of the booths at farmer's market was handing out samples of their fresh almond butter. Yummy! I bought three jars and threw out all the peanut butter. Then I remembered that Delia and I had started one of the latest health fads: twelve to fifteen almonds a day.

Could that be it? Could an allergy to almonds be irritating my heart the same way it was irritating my fingers?

In an ecstasy of insight, I dashed around the house throwing out everything I could find that had them: old bags of trail mix, a couple of almond candy bars, my favorite breakfast granola. When Delia came home, I practically knocked her over in my eagerness. "I think I found it!"

"Found what? What you talking about?"

"I think I found what's causing the AF."

"What do you mean?"

"It's the almonds. I think it's the almonds."

"Are you sure?"

"I'm not sure. But I know how to find out. I'll stop eating them and see what happens."

So I did. As the itchy spot on my fingers slowly faded, the AF seemed to disappear as well. To make sure, I ate almonds again. Back they both came. I stopped. They stopped. I was convinced.

At my next cardiology visit, I said, "I've stopped the atrial fibrillation."

"You've what!?"

"I've been able to stop the fibrillation. It's an allergy to almonds the way I was allergic to peanuts and chocolate as a child."

"How do you know?"

So I told him. I said, "Is there some test we can do to be sure? What if I strap on that little box that records my heart for twenty-four hours?"

"You mean a twenty-four hour halter test?"

"Yeah, that's it. If the AF doesn't show up, will that be enough?"

"I'll schedule it. Come back in two weeks."

Two weeks later, I was back in his office. "The results are positive. I'm taking you off the blood thinner. I think the atrial fibrillation is gone."

I was so excited I almost hugged him. "Wonderful," I said. "We've done it! I can't wait to tell Delia."

Then I thought, *Here's another gift from my past.* As a child, I hadn't liked it when my father insisted I do my homework without his help, but it had taught me to persist until I solved some pretty difficult problems. Now I'd used those skills to solve a problem that may have saved my life.

Things were definitely getting back to normal. My stamina had improved so much I had returned to the woodland trails that wound their way through the nearby hills. As my walks grew longer, I reveled in the fresh earthy smells, the scattered pockets of sunlight, the rich green undergrowth, and the challenge of the climb. Meanwhile I returned to my beloved cello, spending an hour or two each day lost in the rich tones and the urge to improve.

All this was wonderful, yet deep inside something was not yet right. My body was strong and healthy, my mind was no longer depressed, but a part of me still felt empty. Something was missing.

CHAPTER 22

The Wounded Healer

If I can stop one Heart from breaking
I shall not live in vain
If I can ease one Life the Aching
Or cool One Pain

Or help one fainting Robin
Unto his Nest again
I shall not live in Vain.

—*Emily Dickinson*

Ever since my vision quest, my power animal's phrase, "He's mine and I have yet to use him" had haunted me. Rather than drift aimlessly through life, he seemed to be asking me to find ways to act more meaningfully, to look at my choices from a little higher, less selfish, perspective. But how?

Part of the answer had come during my first year of retirement. Adjusting to the loss of structure that work had provided most of my waking life had been difficult. But retirement had also been an opportunity to ask, *What's most important now? Looking back, what were the meaningful experiences in my life? And, if a benevolent God exists, what does he/she want me to do?* Two memories kept pushing forward.

I'm holding my friend, Linda, in a gentle embrace while her whole body shakes, teeth rattling in the warm morning sun. Linda is about to climb an eighteen foot iron-rung ladder fastened to a wall of pink granite and she's scared of heights. I patiently hold her till the shaking stops, then say, "Ready?"

"Just give me another minute."

"Okay."

As I wait, I look down from our perch on a rocky ledge five-hundred feet up a vertical cliff. Far below, early fall wraps a small Maine pond in tones of peach and green, and beyond, a mixed forest of pine, spruce and hardwoods covers the nearby rolling hills. Farther out is the blue Atlantic stretching southeastward to meet the pale sky in a knife-edge horizon. To my left is the lighthouse of my childhood, guardian and protector of the huge bay that stretches for miles inland until its waters disappear behind my left shoulder. Soon I'm lost in the view.

But Linda is not looking. She's holding me tight, eyes closed, facing the granite wall behind me.

Finally she's ready. Taking a deep breath, she places her hands on the ladder rung just above her head. As she takes her first step upward, I immediately follow with my hands one rung below hers. I'm holding my body just outside her body, cradling her in a protective cage that moves with her as we make our way upward. Topping the ladder we carefully make our way along another ledge to the next set of rungs.

"Hold me again." After about three minutes of more shaking followed by a few giggles she says, "I'm ready. Let's do it."

Two weeks before, Linda had told me, "I love our walks together—we go almost everywhere, but not Beehive cliff. You love that climb—you do it every few weeks. I wish I could climb it with you, but I'm too scared."

"Do you really want to go?" I said. "Do you really want to overcome this fear? It's going to be a challenge, but if you want to go, I'll take you."

"How would we do it?"

"I'll make sure we take all the time you need," I said. "I'll hold you whenever you get scared, and we can climb the ladders in a way that will keep you from falling. Once we get onto the ladders it will be better not to turn back, but there are some places before that to test your fears, where turning back is still possible. What do you say? Do you still want to go?"

"Let me think about it."

A week later she said, "Yes, I'll do it, but I want you to promise you will do just what I tell you all the way up."

"Okay," I said, "That should be easy."

"Good. Let's go next week."

After a half-dozen more ladders and a few more halts to shake, cry or gather ourselves, we finally make the top. As we leave the last ladder and move well away from the steep edge, Linda turns, takes in the view for the first time, and starts a little dance of joy. "I did it! I can't believe we've gotten up here! Thank you, *thank* you!"

I'm so pleased I can't stop grinning. *We made it. My plan for getting her up here actually worked. Look how happy she is. This is great!*

*   *   *

It's late afternoon and I'm sitting at my desk at work, finishing up a few chores before going home. I hear a knock and look up. "Hi, Moyha, come on in."

As she closes the door and sits in the chair next to my desk, my friend says, "Tom, is this a good time? Do you have a few minutes?"

"Sure. What can I do?"

"Well, I've got a dear friend who is dying of breast cancer. I want so much to spend time with her during her final weeks but I'm terrified. Death and dying are very scary for me and I don't know what to do. I thought perhaps if you told me the details of Timothy's last two weeks it might help. Would you do that?"

"Of course," I said, "I'd be happy to."

So I told her how everyone had gathered to help us; how people, young and old, had sat with Timothy for hours to keep him company and address his needs; and how his final passing had been so peaceful. After she left, I didn't think any more about it, but three weeks later she was back with a big smile. "Tom, I want to thank you. Everything went so well. I was able to sit with my dying friend for a couple of hours each day, all the way through to the end. Sometimes I held her hand, sometimes we talked a little, but most of the time I just sat with her. And when our tears came, they came easily. It was very moving. Again, thank you."

"But, Moyha, I didn't do anything. I just told you about Timothy."

"Yes, but that made all the difference."

As I did the last of my chores before heading home, I realized that the dull ordinary day at the office had turned much brighter. I had to suppress the nutty desire to skip as I walked down the hall and out into the parking lot.

Were these two experiences examples of what the power animal of my vision quest had asked of me?

*   *   *

The year that I retired, I attended a variety of workshops in shamanism, eventually entering Michael Harner's three-year program of advanced study[30]. Much of this training was about the shaman's traditional role as healer. Soon friends and acquaintances began coming to me for help. I would listen, then journey on their behalf. In the journey I would meet with a teacher or power animal, tell them about the client, then do as instructed, often with interesting results.

I remember one in particular. In it, the journey teacher said, "Here's a robin and a rabbit. I want you to take them to your client."

"But," I said, "if this guy needs a power animal, it needs to be really powerful. He needs a lion or a tiger—something fierce and protective, something that will give him confidence."

"No. You are to bring back this robin and this rabbit. Do as I tell you."

"All right," I said, "I'll do it. But they're so wimpy. I think he needs something tougher."

When the journey was over, I told my client what had happened. "I never told you about my first wife who died a few years ago," he said. "I have missed her a great deal. Her name was Robin, and she was exactly as you describe. You also didn't know that we called each other 'Bunny.'"

After surgery I hadn't felt powerful enough to continue the work, so I had stopped. But I always learned something from clients, and helping them brought a warm glow similar to that of those two Maine memories. However, there was an important difference. Journeying for clients only worked when I stepped out of the way and became a hollow bone, letting the drum empty me of self. It was the teachers and power animals of non-ordinary reality that did the work, not me.

On the other hand, climbing Beehive with Linda and telling Tim's story to Moyha had been, not from the place of the hollow bone, but rather from a direct expression of who *I* was. Helping as I had, had brought forth my better self. I liked that better self and wanted more. At the same time, helping them had been so easy! Wasn't doing something significant supposed to be difficult?

---

[30] see www.shamanism.org

It reminded me of an allegory my friend, Joe, had told me a few weeks after retirement . . .

Jakub's Story

Jakub was the mayor of a small town in Czechoslovakia. As a successful businessman, he donated some of his considerable wealth to the community. The townspeople thanked him by naming first a school and later a village thoroughfare after him. Each time he passed the school or drove down the street, he sat a little taller, proud of this outward sign of his generosity. It had been hard to give, but he knew he must for his standing in the community.

In the prime of his life, Jakub was struck down by a heart attack and soon found himself just outside Saint Peter's gate. As he strode forward, head tall, he thought, "I've done all the right things. Saint Peter will surely let me in."

But Saint Peter stopped him. "Slow down Jakub. Not so fast. We're not sure you belong here yet."

"What do you mean? I've been a good man. I've donated generously to many causes. Isn't that enough?"

"But Jakub," Saint Peter replied, "Why weren't you Jakub? Go back and be the 'you' that God made you to be."

In order to be truly me, I would have to change a lot of old habits. Most of my days now were spent either lying around waiting to get better, or full of a million distractions that cluttered my life. Things were going to have to get much simpler if this authentic self was going to have any room to breathe. It reminded me of an email someone had sent, one I had almost tossed months before . . .

The Sultan and the Elephant Sculptor

Once upon a time there was a Sultan and a Master Sculptor. The sculptor was revered by all in the Sultan's kingdom for his exquisite renderings of elephants. Each elephant was carved with such vitality that the image seemed to leap from the stone as alive and vibrant as the living, breathing creature it represented.

One day the Sultan sent for the sculptor. "Master Sculptor, I want you to carve for me the biggest and most magnificent elephant ever."

"Sire," replied the sculptor, "bring me the largest block of marble that can be found in your quarries and we'll see what happens."

An enormous block of white marble was delivered to the sculptor's work yard where it sat untouched for more than a year. Finally the Sultan got impatient and again called for the sculptor. "Master Sculptor, you promised to create for me the most magnificent elephant in all the land but when I ride by your work yard I see nothing."

"Sire, perhaps you misunderstood. I do not create anything. Rather, my job is to be patient—to discover what awaits us deep in the stone. Once the creature is revealed, my job is to remove all the pieces of stone that are not elephant in order to lay bare the essence that is."

Like the elephant sculptor, I would need to strip away a lot to make room for what I wanted. But if helping others was what I wanted, how would I go about it? Those two experiences in Maine had just appeared out of the blue. They hadn't been planned. Then I thought of one of the poems I had discovered a couple of years after retirement:

The Bright Field

I have seen the sun break through
to illuminate a small field
for a while, and gone my way
and forgotten it. But that was the pearl
of great price, the one field that had
the treasure in it. I realize now
that I must give all that I have
to possess it. Life is not hurrying

on to a receding future, nor hankering after
an imagined past. It is the turning
aside like Moses to the miracle
of the lit bush, to a brightness
that seemed as transitory as your youth
once, but is the eternity that awaits you.

—*R. S. Thomas*

Were opportunities to help others the Pearl of Great Price?

Then I remembered other messages from the vision quest. What had the tree said, the one that marked the east boundary of my vision quest site? "Become a mentor for those needing guidance. Listen with love to those in grief and pain."

Could I learn to see each opportunity the moment it arose, turning aside from my headlong rush through life, "like Moses to the miracle of the lit bush"? I certainly wasn't in any rush now. I was spending most of my day lying around feeling sorry for myself. Maybe it would be easier than I thought.

All through my preparations for surgery and its aftermath, friends kept in touch, wanting to know how I was progressing. The more I told them, the more they wanted more details. Sometimes a simple, "Hello, how are you?" became an hour's conversation. Soon friends began referring other friends:

"I have someone who has to have valve surgery much like yours. He's pretty scared. Would you talk to him?"

"My friend's wife has just discovered she has breast cancer and he's freaked. Can he call you?"

"Dorothy is recovering from heart valve surgery but it's taking a long time and she's getting discouraged. Could you pay her a visit?"

One Sunday after Quaker Meeting, I had been standing near three women, half listening to their conversation. One, a slight acquaintance of mine, was telling the others about the sudden death of a family member just the day before. There had been the briefest moment in her narration when I knew she was ready to be held and, without thinking, I had responded. For ten minutes I held her while she sobbed into my shoulder. Slowly I was learning how to see those quick flashes in the bright field and to "turn aside" instead of hesitating past the moment of possibility.

Much of what I was doing I had learned with co-counseling—how to listen, how to be present, how to care effectively, but that had been within the bounds and rules of a formal session. This, however, was new and different. Here there were no rules. Instead I began to draw on my intuition and a long, rich life. Experiences like Chris' illness, Timothy's death, the loss of my parents, and my own illness had given me an intimate and empathetic understanding of fear and pain and loss, an understanding that allowed me to listen deeply and well.

The more I opened to this possibility for service, the more people appeared. Some wanted to learn from my experiences, but most just needed to talk. Sometimes, after listening for many minutes, I would say something to honor their struggle or praise them for their efforts. Some would speak as though I were the lost loved one, expressing for the first time things that had never been said. Once, by listening carefully, I was able to whisper what they had been waiting a lifetime to hear. Another paused after a long narration and said, "I don't know why I'm talking to you like this. I've never spoken of this to anyone, not even myself."

So many people had given of themselves when I had been in trouble. Now it was a gift to give a little in return. The open heart surgery had opened my heart wide, giving me new purpose: the opportunity to become what shamans call "a wounded healer."

CHAPTER 23

The Illuminated Heart

Love After Love

The time will come
when, with elation,
you will greet yourself arriving
at your own door, in your own mirror,
and each will smile at the other's welcome,

and say, sit here. Eat.
You will love again the stranger who was your self.
Give wine. Give bread. Give back your heart
to itself, to the stranger who has loved you

all your life, whom you ignored
for another, who knows you by heart.
Take down the love letters from the bookshelf,

the photographs, the desperate notes,
peel your own image from the mirror.
Sit. Feast on your life.

—Derek Walcott

Shortly after returning home from the hospital I sent a newsy email to various friends scattered around the country. In two or three pages I outlined the events of the previous months, including some of my struggles with fear and my efforts to find meaning. I received many friendly, supportive replies, with one unexpected recurring theme: "Can I forward this email to my Dad / friend / neighbor? They're going through a similar crisis and need to hear your story." Then my local friends took up the refrain: "You have something important to say. You should write about your experiences." This was flattering, but I had no training and didn't see myself as a writer, so I ignored their suggestions.

One Saturday morning at farmer's market, I stopped to chat with Ken. Ken doesn't just sell fresh organic mushrooms and green sprouts. He also provides a sharp mind, a listening ear, and vibrant conversation. While his hands made change for other customers, he asked penetrating questions that drew out new details of my story. Finally, as I paused for breath, he said the now familiar words, "You should communicate this to a broader audience."

"Ken, that's what everyone's been saying, but I'm not a writer. I can babble on and on okay, but write? That's a different story."

"But Tom, you really should. You've something important to say, something that many people are desperate to hear. A lot of people have had life-threatening surgery, but few have addressed these fundamental issues the way you have."

"You really think it's that important?"

"I do."

"Okay, I'll think about it. Maybe I'll do an outline, just to see what might be there."

When I got home, I helped Delia unload the groceries, then sat at my desk. Three hours and eight pages of outline later I paused: *Maybe Ken's right. Maybe there is something here.*

So I started. My first attempts were atrocious—halting half-sentences full of cliché and bromide, without an ounce of story or dialogue. The more I struggled the more I felt the way Pablo Neruda must have felt in his poem *La Poesia*: "I didn't know what to say, my mouth / could not speak, / my eyes could not see . . . ." So I signed up for a once-a-week writing class. Slowly I improved. But squeezing out the necessary words was agony and there were whole sections where I couldn't seem to get it right, no matter how I tried.

Then, about a year into the project, something shifted. The rest of Neruda's poem captures it well: " . . . and something ignited in my soul, / fever or unremembered wings / and I went my own way, / deciphering that burning fire / and I wrote the first bare line, / bare, without substance, pure / foolishness, / pure wisdom / and suddenly I saw / the heavens / unfasten and open."

To articulate each experience I had to get uncomfortably close to it. I had to tease each moment apart, burrow under its skin, dive through muscle, walk through bone. Only when I approached the very heart of it, the very center of its truth, did the writing begin to sing. Now all the pieces began to take shape. For the first time I could see, in one place and time, all these disparate elements: the shy, scared little boy; the frozen, ineffectual parent; the lover of wild places; the scientist and shaman; the vision-quester; the terrified heart patient; and the listener/mentor. Even the parts rejected long ago as too painful or childish, now contributed to the whole. And, as the book took shape, so I came to a new wholeness, an inner harmony I had not experienced before.

Then I remembered one of those magic mornings with Mary Ann a couple of months after surgery. We had just finished our journeys and she was putting on her coat to leave. As she stepped to the door she said, "Tom, look. On the altar. The red heart on your Peruvian flute is all lit up." As I moved closer I could see a bright spot of rainbow highlighting the heart, lifting it off the flute in a glowing ecstasy of color. "It's the morning sun coming through the prism in the window."

"How beautiful," I said. "With heart surgery so recent, perhaps it means something, but I don't have a clue what that might be."

Now, with the writing coming to a close, I understood. Wrapped in this glowing, illuminated heart was a symbol for all the richness and meaning of this experience.

AFTER THOUGHTS

Christopher is now 41 and doing well. Julie has returned to her beloved Montana ranch. Sarah at 37 also live in Montana with her son Munro, and Tamara, who's now 39, lives in California.

APPENDICES

APPENDIX A

George Davis Snell

Honors and Awards
1952   Elected to American Academy of Arts and Sciences
1955   Hekteon Medal of American Medical Association
1962   Griffen Animal Care Panel Award
1962   Bertner Foundation Award
1967   Gregor Mendel Medal, Czechoslovak Academy of Sciences
1970   Elected to National Academy of Sciences
1971   Paul Ehrlich Medal—International Immunology Conference
1976   Gairdner Foundation Award
1978   National Cancer Institute Award
1978   Elected to British Transplantation Society, Honorary
1978   Wolf Prize in Medicine
1978   Institut de France (medal)
1979   Elected to French Academy of Sciences, Foreign Associate
1980   National Library of Medicine award
1980   Nobel Prize in Physiology or Medicine
1982   Elected to American Philosophical Society
1983   Elected to British Society of Immunology, Honorary
Numerous honorary degrees, mostly in the 1980s and early 1990s.
George Snell's autobiography can be found on the web at http://nobelprize.
org/nobel_prizes/medicine/laureates/1980/snell-autobio.html

APPENDIX B

Making Prayer Ties

To make a circle of prayer ties, take a small pinch of ceremonial tobacco and "place" a prayer in it. This is traditionally done by holding the tobacco against your forehead, closing your eyes, and thinking the prayer into the tobacco. Now place the tobacco into the center of a two-inch square of colored cotton cloth. Traditional colors might be red, white, black and yellow, but this can vary from tribe to tribe.

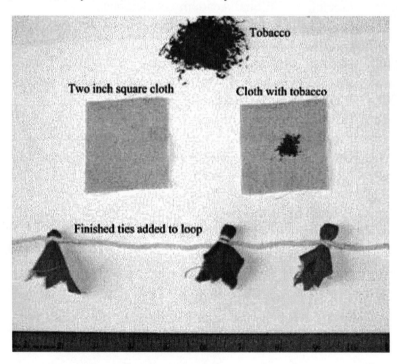

"Wrap the cloth around the tobacco so it looks like this:

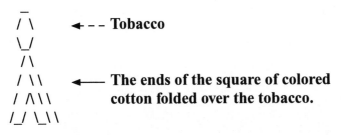

```
 _
/ \      ◄ - - Tobacco
\_/
/ \
/ \\     ◄──── The ends of the square of colored
/ /\\\           cotton folded over the tobacco.
/_/ \_\\
```

Tie the wrapped tobacco into a large circle of cotton string, using interlocking loops to form a special knot called a clove hitch.

The Clove Hitch for fastening Prayer Ties

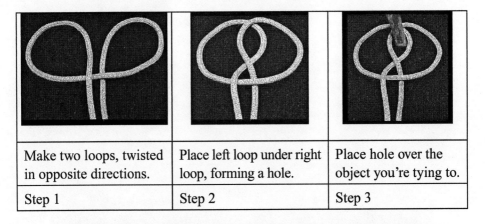

Make two loops, twisted in opposite directions.	Place left loop under right loop, forming a hole.	Place hole over the object you're tying to.
Step 1	Step 2	Step 3

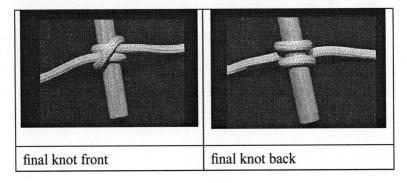

final knot front	final knot back

Keep adding ties for as many prayers as you wish.

The symbolic beauty of the clove hitch is that, although it fastens the prayer tie to the string, it doesn't actually create a knot. If you were to remove the tie, the string would fall free without any snags, keeping the circle pure. You can also add ties at any point in the circle, where an ordinary knot would require the ends to the string to be free.

APPENDIX C

Shamanism

Shamanic journeying is a joyful path to regaining the knowledge of how to bring our lives back into a place of harmony and balance. It helps us to wake up to our full creative potential.

Sandra Ingerman

S hamanism is ancient, with signs of it first appearing as much as 40,000 years ago. It has cropped up again and again across very diverse cultures and in widely dispersed areas across the globe. Our ancient ancestors discovered how to maximize human abilities of mind and spirit for healing and problem-solving. The methods they developed is today known as "shamanism," a term that comes from a Siberian tribal word for its practitioners: "shaman" (pronounced SHAH-mahn). Shamans are a type of medicine man or woman distinguished by the use of journeys to hidden worlds otherwise known mainly through myth, dream, and near-death experiences. Most commonly they do this by entering an altered state of consciousness using monotonous percussive sound such as with a drum or rattle. The shamanic practitioner travels to these non-ordinary realities to gain information or healing for an individual or a community. The "information" may be presented in the form of advice, guidance, spiritual healing, enlightenment, or assistance in decision-making or problem-solving. It aids in returning people to harmony. It can be transformative.

The expression of Shamanism in each culture has been unique to that culture, but underlying that diversity is a universal commonality. That common thread, in today's world, is what Michael Harner[31] calls "core shamanism".

---

[31]   Dr. Michael Harner—anthropologist, teacher, workshop leader, and founder of The Foundation for Shamanic Studies (www.shamanism.org)

APPENDIX D

Religious Society of Friends (Quakers)

The spiritual search that led me to the Quakers started early. When I was small, my dad told me about my namesake, Great, Great Grandfather Thomas Snell. A preacher, he began his work in a church in North Brookfield, Massachusetts in 1797 and continued his ministry there for sixty-four years. Reading about him in my grandmother's family history greatly impressed my young mind. If he was my namesake, would I become a minister like him? What would that be like?

When I was a little older, I started Sunday school, first in my mother's Episcopal church (her father had been the minister in nearby Southwest Harbor), then, a few years later, at the Congregational church where my dad sang in the choir. I liked Sunday school, especially the Bible stories such as Joseph and the coat of many colors, Moses parting the waters of the Red Sea, or the Good Samaritan.

But as I grew older I became dissatisfied. I couldn't seem to believe like everyone else. It didn't make sense to my rational mind that Jesus could rise from the dead. It didn't make sense that anyone could be divine, no matter what the Bible said. I couldn't see that Jesus was anything more than an amazing man who had discovered some deep and important truths about how to live. I wanted to learn what he might teach me, but it didn't seem divine. For every miracle I would think, "There's got to be some explanation. Maybe Lazarus wasn't dead. Maybe he was only in a coma and woke when Jesus went to him." I began to nickname myself "Doubting Thomas." So when the minister gave his sermon each Sunday I silently rebelled.

But I was still yearning, still looking for something I couldn't grasp, couldn't put words to but felt should be there. One high school summer I went to a different church each Sunday, sat through the sermon, and went away dissatisfied.

Finally, in the spring of my freshman year in college, I wandered up the lilac-lined path and into the door of the Quaker Meeting house that stood at one corner of the campus. I stepped into a simple room—no cross, no altar, no adornments. Instead there were three concentric circles of chairs so that people could face each other across a plain open area. The room was nearly full, but I was able to find a seat. Then I waited . . . and waited . . . and waited . . . *When is the service going to start?* I looked around. Everyone seemed at ease. Most had their eyes closed—some let their gaze move gently around the room. But nothing happened. Everyone just sat in silence. Finally, after about twenty minutes, I heard the squeak of someone shifting in a chair. I looked up in time to see an old gentleman stand up. For a moment he seemed to gather himself. Then he spoke a few words and sat down. Again a long silence and again the creak of another chair, this time a young woman. She, too, spoke briefly, her voice so soft and hesitant I could barely hear her. After a pause a middle aged woman with a commanding voice spoke at some length before sitting. As the silence settled over the room again, I felt a shift inside. Now I welcomed the quiet, almost like an old friend that I had forgotten long ago and almost lost. Sitting there, I thought about what had been said, and how the three messages, although quite different, had a common thread. Suddenly the people on either side of me reached over and shook my hand. I looked up and saw that everyone was shaking hands. It was over.

This was so different. These weren't preachers with a prepared Sunday sermon; they were people like me, speaking from the heart as though God were talking directly through them. After a few more visits, I knew I had found my spiritual home.

When individuals stood up in Meeting, they spoke of many things, but two strongly recurring themes were peace and service. Many of the men were pacifists and spoke out against war and violence. Others worked to address social issues like poverty and famine, both locally and around the world. These people weren't just talking, they were acting, whether through organizations like The American Friends Service Committee (AFSC) or Friends Committee on National Legislation (FCNL), or were part of local peace vigils, marches, or volunteer efforts to help the poor or disadvantaged. It was through their example that my first wife, Julie, and I joined the staff of the Meeting School and spent eight years there in Quaker service.

PERMISSIONS

*G*rateful acknowledgement is made to the following for permission to reprint selections included in this book:

Permission to use front and back cover art granted by the artist, Robert Phipps, of Bar Harbor, ME.

From THE INFERNO by Dante Alighieri, translated by Robert and Jean Hollander, Canto I, lines 1-9. Copyright © 2002 by Robert Hollander and Jean Hollander. Used by permission of Doubleday, a division of Random House, Inc.

Non-exclusive permission to use the stories of Christopher, Timothy, and myself as expressed in your manuscript is freely given. Julia M. Childs (formerly Julie Snell)

Lord, I am but a flit of a butterfly wing . . . Copyright © Rachel Medlock. Used by her permission.

Suspended by Denise Levertov, from EVENING TRAIN, copyright © by Denise Levertov. Reprinted by permission of New Directions Publishing Corp.

The Summer Day from *House of Light* by Mary Oliver. Copyright © 1990 by Mary Oliver. Reprinted by permission of Beacon Press, Boston.

Excerpt from HASTEN SLOWLY: *The Journey of Sir Laurens van der Post,* by Mickey Lemle. Used with permission from Lemle Pictures, Inc., www. lemlepictures.com.

Louisa May Alcott, *Work, a Story of Experience.* p. 202. Penguin Classics, 1994 edition. First published in book form in 1873 by Roberts Brothers of Boston. (copyright expired)

Quoted from: *The Camelot Project,* The University of Rochester (http://www.lib. rochester.edu/camelot/cphome.stm). Copyright © Alan Lupack and Barbara Tepa Lupack. All original material in the project, unless otherwise indicated, is copyright © Alan Lupack.